FIRST EDITION PUBLISHED 2012

The Write Design Press

DEDICATION

To any content creator who has ever been attacked by Blogger's Block, Writer's Block, or any other Creative Block.

ACKNOWLEDGEMENTS

A GREAT, BIG THANK YOU to everyone who supported me on my book writing journey, from the suggestion to write the book, to the crowdfunding campaign, to the final product.

My family and friends. I know they are tired of listening to me talk about writing, blogging, and social media, but they do a good job of faking like they're listening.

Internet Coach Vernessa Taylor. There are no expressions of gratitude that compare to having someone to care about you and what you do. I thank Vernessa for being my accountability partner and for keeping me in order.

My editorial team: Tasha Clopton Stubbs, President of TLCS Productions, and Charisse Smiley-Chambers, owner of Edit this? Edit That! Both ladies were committed to the highest standards of writing and would not accept anything less.

Sabryna Washington, the creative genius behind Ingenuity7. I appreciate her patience, professionalism and outstanding graphic design and marketing skills.

To everyone who pre-ordered my published book and companion guide; who gave me words of encouragement, advice, feedback and resources; and who prayed for me.

Big hugs to the donors of my crowdfunding campaign who made the completion of this project possible:

Dr. Bernadette Anderson
Aisha Ato
Alice Boswell
McKinley Brown
Ted Bryant
John Cook
Dr. Sarah Crawley
Kelley Dowell
KeriLynn Engel
Clara Freeman
Doneice Fuzzell
Rodney Giordani
Dante Hamilton
Lewis Harris
Verlene Hill
Dequiana Jackson
Dennis Johnson
Dorothy Keller
Maria Martinez
Cedric McCay
Allison McCray
William Miles
Otis Monroe
Marc Moran
Rick Nelson
Stephen Pore
Queen Searles
Christina Stringfellow
Kareen Tolliver
Talawn Unger Jackson
Margo Watson
Theodore Whittier

And most importantly, I have to thank God for giving me the vision, courage, direction and resources to make this all happen.

DON'T MISS OUT, SIGN UP TODAY

To link to the actual posts in each of the categories,
go to www.overcomingbloggersblock.com to sign up for updates.

TABLE OF CONTENTS

INTRODUCTION

If you are reading this book, it is assumed that you have experienced blogger's block at some point in your life, and it has either hindered you from starting or continuing on your blogging journey.

What is Blogger's Block?

This is a common ailment among content creators of all types. You know what you want to do; you are ready to do it; but the spirit of creativity is against you. That spirit either leaves you completely or plays tricks with your mind by changing the direction of your initial ideas which, in fact, is another form of blockage. You often become overwhelmed and do nothing.

Why Do You Get Blogger's Block?

Because you're human. (This is as scientific as it gets.)

What are the Symptoms?

- You draw a total blank when you are ready to create
- Your creativity is suddenly zapped away for no apparent reason, interrupting your creative flow
- Your mind plays tricks on you

Side Effects

- Frustration
- Tears
- Screaming
- Disbelief
- Lack of productivity
- Hair pulling (your own or someone else's)
- Describe other effects here:

The two most damaging side effects of this horrible condition are:
1. You never start blogging
2. You stop blogging completely

Thus, this book was created to prepare you for those times when Blogger's Block attacks.

SOLUTIONS

1. Breathe
2. Take a break
3. Flip through this book for inspiration
4. Walk away
5. Watch or read something positive
6. Brainstorm ideas using the 62 Blog Posts to Overcome Blogger's Block companion guide
7. Lay down
8. Listen to mellow music
9. Hang out on social networking and news sites
10. Visit Overcoming Blogger's Block website for topic ideas

HOW TO USE THIS BOOK

For blog post categories that have one visual sample, the page setup is shown below:

Left Page	Right Page
▪ Explanation of the type of blog post ▪ Pros and other considerations for creating that particular post	▪ Visual sample of the type of post

For categories that have two visual samples, there is a blank page to ensure consistency throughout the book. Use this page to take notes, jot ideas, or draft action plans.

Disclaimer

The sites presented in this book were selected for two reasons:

1. It is apparent that the owners and managers of these sites are passionate and committed to providing valuable and quality content to their readers
2. The individual post or the entire site best represented the specific blog post category

Note: Some sites have been shut down since I started my book in 2012. Others have not been updated in a while. The blog posts presented are still relevant today.

I hope you enjoy working the lessons in this book as much as I have enjoyed producing them for you. Be sure to purchase the 62 Blog Posts to Overcome Blogger's Block Companion Guide to activate your creative flow through brainstorming and journaling.

Happy creating!!

COMPANION WORKBOOK

To help you generate creative blog posts ideas, a companion workbook is available. Visit www.overcomingbloggersblock.com for more details.

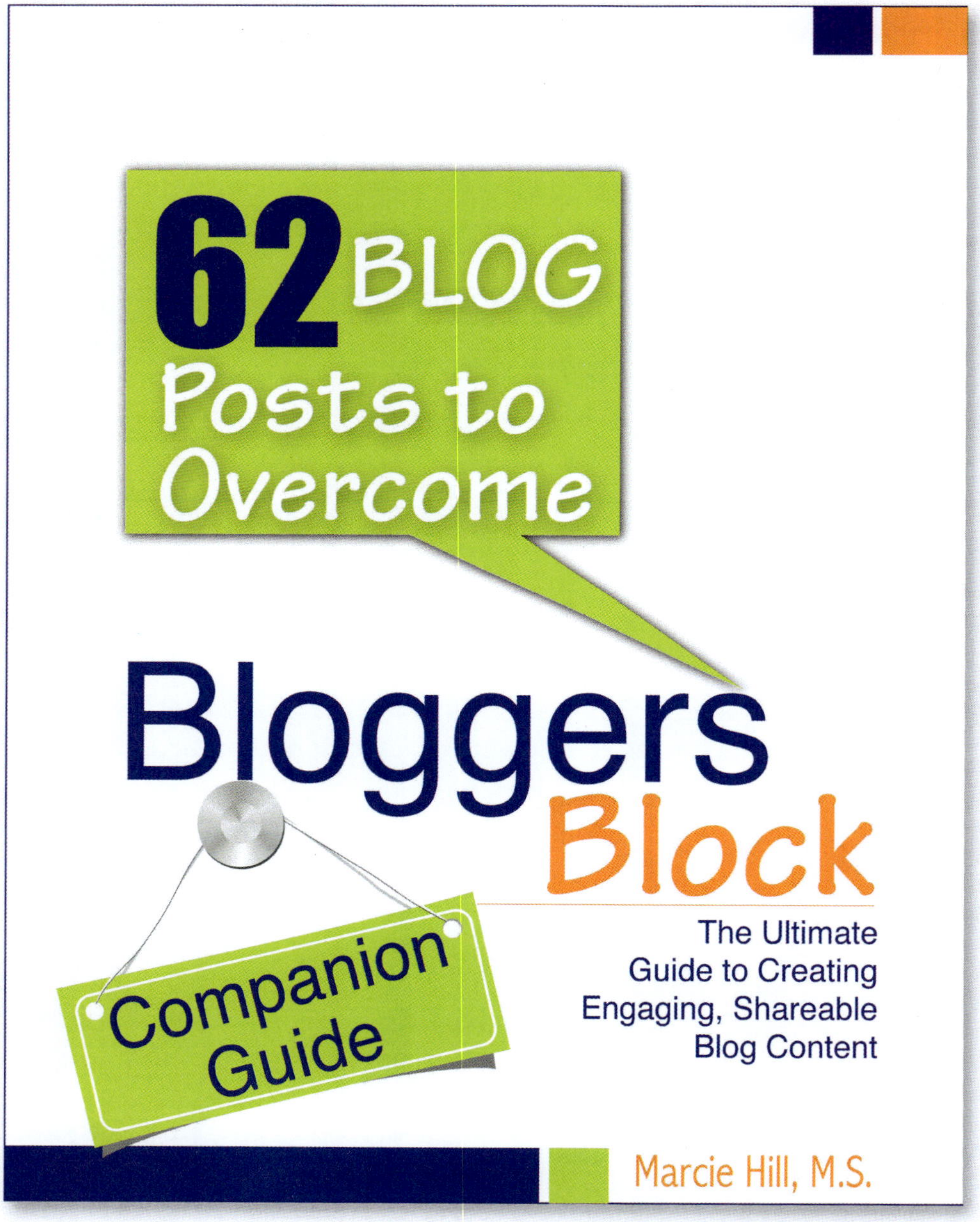

PART 1
MOST POPULAR POSTS

There are ten types of blog posts that are considered popular because they are found on most sites you visit. They are also preferred because they are easy for bloggers to write, easy for readers to scan, and they tend to rank high on search engines. They are:

1. **How-To**
2. **Quick Tips/Quick Reference**
3. **Definition**
4. **Informational**
5. **Stories**
6. **Inspirational**
7. **Research**
8. **Lists**
9. **Checklists**
10. **Link Posts**

#1 HOW-TO

Teach your audience how to make their lives easier and better through How-To posts or tutorials. These instructional posts provide step-by-step instructions, as well as tips and solutions on how to do or attain something. When you write this this type of blog post, you can share things that your audience already knows or you can simply add to their knowledge base.

Audio clips, images, videos, and presentations are engaging and interactive tools that you can use to instruct your audience. To get topic ideas or to learn how to write How-To posts, check other blogs, forums, and even messages that come to your e-mail inbox. Use the things that appeal to you and discard the rest.

Pros:

- How-To posts rank high in popular blog post types
- They are one of the easiest ways to build your expertise and your brand

Other Considerations:

- Remember, you want to make things easier and better for the readers, so make sure your instructions are clear, organized, and do not include unnecessary steps
- Don't confuse your audience by discussing too many topics.
- While How-To posts are very tempting to write and easy for your audience to read, be sure to vary the types of posts that you produce on your site
- You can also put a spin on your posts by sharing How ***Not*** To do things in creative ways. For example, instead of writing "How to Make Friends on Facebook," you can write "How Not to Make Friends on Facebook."

SAMPLE HOW-TO POST

This post from CoachNotes Blog by Vernessa Taylor is the perfect How-To post. She gives an explanation of what FlowPlayer video is, what it does, and highlights some of its features. She also provides images that show exactly what readers can expect to see as they perform each step.

#2 QUICK TIPS/QUICK REFERENCE

Quick Tips or Quick References are similar to How-to posts because they tell people how to do something impactful in just a few steps. For instance, a How-To post may read: "Write Your Book in 10 Days." A Quick Tip post would read: "Write Your Book in 10 Days in Three Easy Steps." These tips could be written as a list or in narrative format. You can also use multimedia tools to show your audience how to do things.

Pro:

- Quick Posts are generally easy to create depending on the topic. You can even summarize topics from your archives

Other Considerations:

- Make sure the tips will enrich your readers' lives
- Create Quick Tips and Quick Reference posts by putting a different twist on content you have already created online and offline

SAMPLE QUICK TIPS POST

Ben Barden's site, Quick Blog Tips, provides a wide range of information on how to enhance your blog's online and offline visibility in just a few steps.

In the post below, Ben outlines six things you can do to make your posts really stand out, which will ultimately keep people returning to your site. Some of these things will require you to step out of your comfort zone and put your full self into your blog posts.

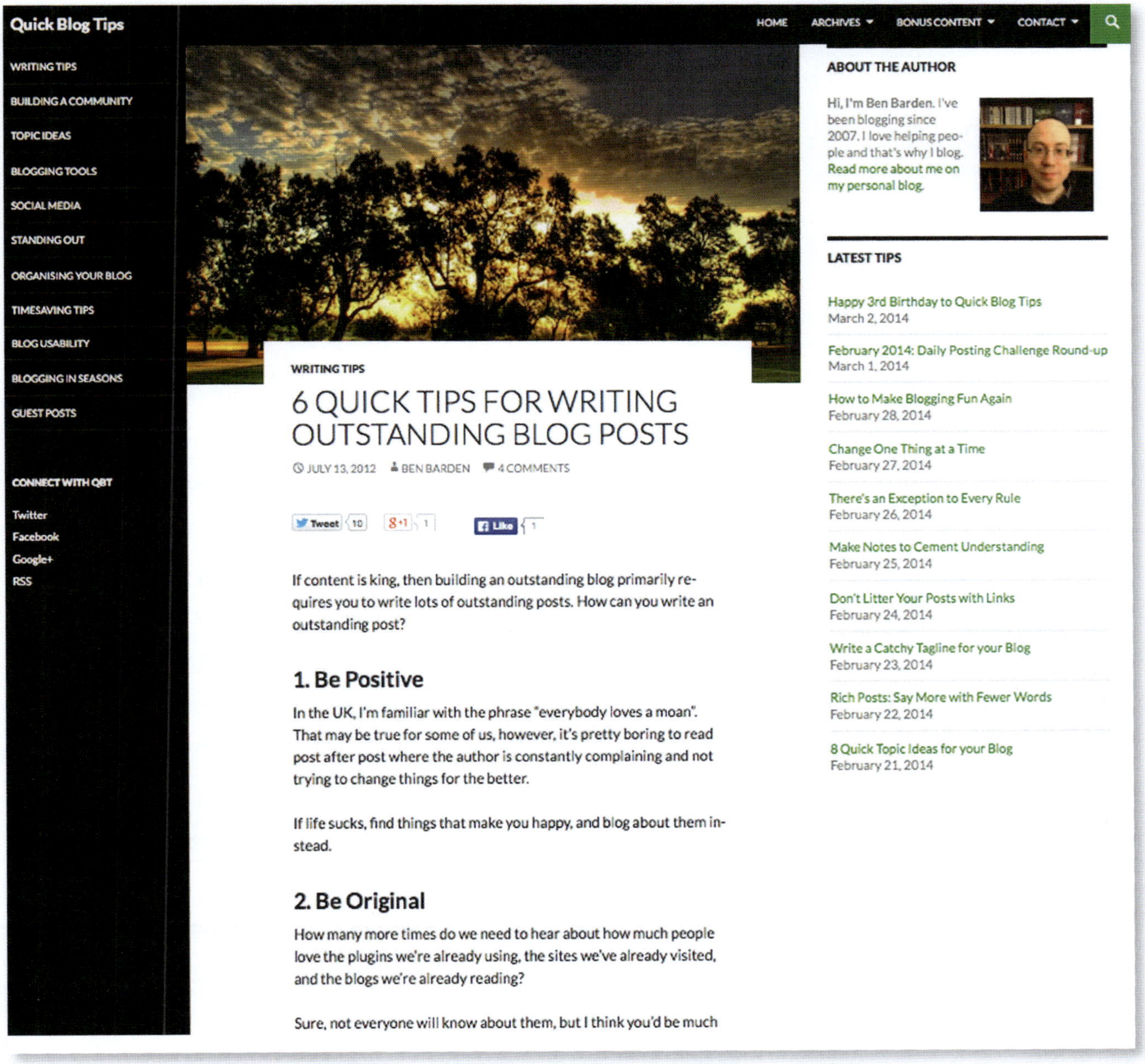

#3 DEFINITION

Definition posts either introduce new terms and concepts to readers or they make the concepts simple for them to understand. This can be done using text, audio, video, images, or presentations.

Pros:

- You are translating technical terms and jargon into everyday language
- Both your audience's knowledge base and your teaching ability will increase

Other Considerations:

- Be engaging and use a conversational tone when relaying information to avoid making your readers feel like you are talking down to them or that you are undermining their intelligence
- Be sure to answer all of your audience's questions

SAMPLE DEFINITION POST

As you can see on my business site, The Write Design Company, I introduced my audience to live blogging. Specifically, I defined what it is, how it is similar to Twitter, and how it differs from traditional blogging. Because live blogging is sharing information in real-time, you can add an extra level of interactivity with your audience by providing details from conferences, networking events, educational sessions, and other events in which they may be interested.

the Write Design Company

Search this website ... SEARCH

Home | Services | Overcome Blogger's Block! | Blog | Contact | About TWDC

Get E-mail Updates

Enter your email address:

Subscribe

Delivered by FeedBurner

Our Specialties

- Blog
- Blogging
- Classes & Workshops
- Content Creation
- Conversations
- Corporate Training
- Events
- General Business
- Interviews
- Live Blogging
- Opportunities
- Reports
- Resources
- Reviews
- Social Media

You are here: Home » Blog » **Day 1: What is Live Blogging?**

Day 1: What is Live Blogging?

JULY 5, 2011 BY MARCIE HILL LEAVE A COMMENT

WRITE NOW!

Whenever I tell people that The Write Design Company offers live blogging services, there are three questions I get:

1. What is live blogging?
2. Is it like Twitter?
3. What is the difference between blogging and live blogging?

Here are the answers to all of those questions.

What is Live Blogging?

Live blogging is real-time reporting. Event details are shared as they unfold.

Live Blogging vs. Twitter?

Twitter is the most popular microblogging program which allows you to blog up to 140 characters in real-time. Live blogging allows for more characters, and it integrates Twitter, photos, videos, audio. It also easily connects with other social sites like Facebook and YouTube.

#4 INFORMATIONAL

Generally speaking, all blog posts are informational because all bloggers have the common goal of educating their audiences. These posts could be as simple as a definition article or as in-depth as a webinar.

There are three ways to educate your audience in an informational post:

1. Introduce your audience to new terms, concepts, ideas, and resources
2. Add new twists to old topics
3. Put an engaging spin on an otherwise boring topic

Pros:

- These posts will boost your credibility as a resource and as an authority
- You will increase your knowledge base by learning from your research and from your readers' responses

Other Considerations:

- Make your explanations as engaging as possible to avoid boring your audience
- Use multimedia tools when possible

SAMPLE INFORMATIONAL POST

Ms. Ileane is passionate about teaching her audience how to use social media and multimedia tools on Basic Blog Tips. In the comprehensive post below, she used text and video to relay information and then provided links to different sources.

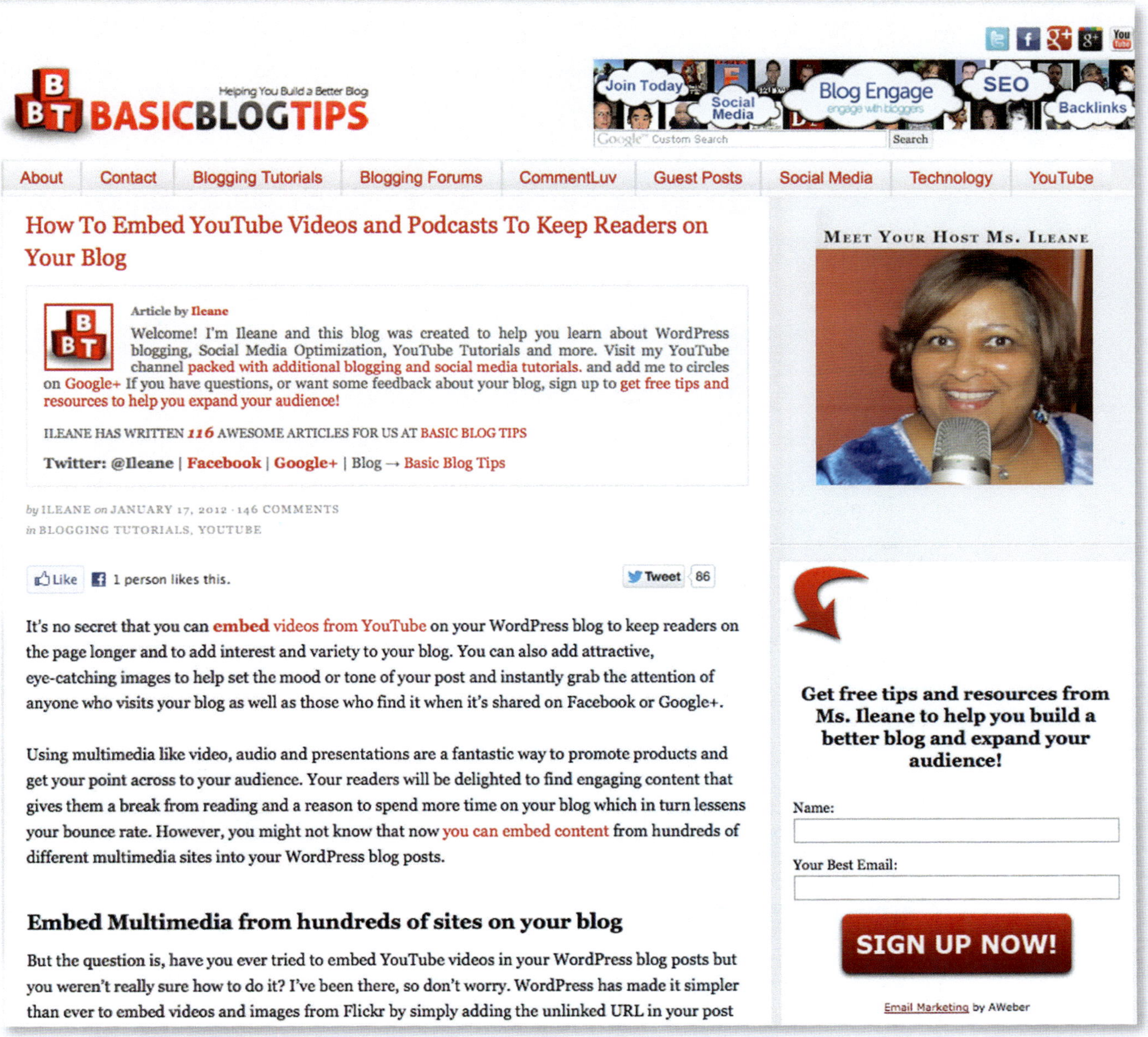

How To Embed YouTube Videos and Podcasts To Keep Readers on Your Blog

Article by Ileane

Welcome! I'm Ileane and this blog was created to help you learn about WordPress blogging, Social Media Optimization, YouTube Tutorials and more. Visit my YouTube channel packed with additional blogging and social media tutorials. and add me to circles on Google+ If you have questions, or want some feedback about your blog, sign up to get free tips and resources to help you expand your audience!

ILEANE HAS WRITTEN 116 AWESOME ARTICLES FOR US AT BASIC BLOG TIPS

Twitter: @Ileane | Facebook | Google+ | Blog → Basic Blog Tips

by ILEANE on JANUARY 17, 2012 · 146 COMMENTS
in BLOGGING TUTORIALS, YOUTUBE

Like 1 person likes this. Tweet 86

It's no secret that you can embed videos from YouTube on your WordPress blog to keep readers on the page longer and to add interest and variety to your blog. You can also add attractive, eye-catching images to help set the mood or tone of your post and instantly grab the attention of anyone who visits your blog as well as those who find it when it's shared on Facebook or Google+.

Using multimedia like video, audio and presentations are a fantastic way to promote products and get your point across to your audience. Your readers will be delighted to find engaging content that gives them a break from reading and a reason to spend more time on your blog which in turn lessens your bounce rate. However, you might not know that now you can embed content from hundreds of different multimedia sites into your WordPress blog posts.

Embed Multimedia from hundreds of sites on your blog

But the question is, have you ever tried to embed YouTube videos in your WordPress blog posts but you weren't really sure how to do it? I've been there, so don't worry. WordPress has made it simpler than ever to embed videos and images from Flickr by simply adding the unlinked URL in your post

#5 STORIES

Everyone has a story. Everyone loves hearing stories, especially those with lessons and happy endings. Share your experiences and lessons learned on your site and encourage your readers to do the same.

Pros:

- Your readers will get to know you better, which will keep them returning to your site
- You will get to know your readers better, which will help build your relationship with them online and offline

Other Consideration:

- Don't get too personal. People want to get to know you, but not like *THAT*

SAMPLE STORY POST

Authentic Woman is a site where women and men can share their stories of "becoming" who they are. We all go through things in life that make us stronger, wiser, and more in-tune with our purpose. Clara Freeman created this site just for that reason.

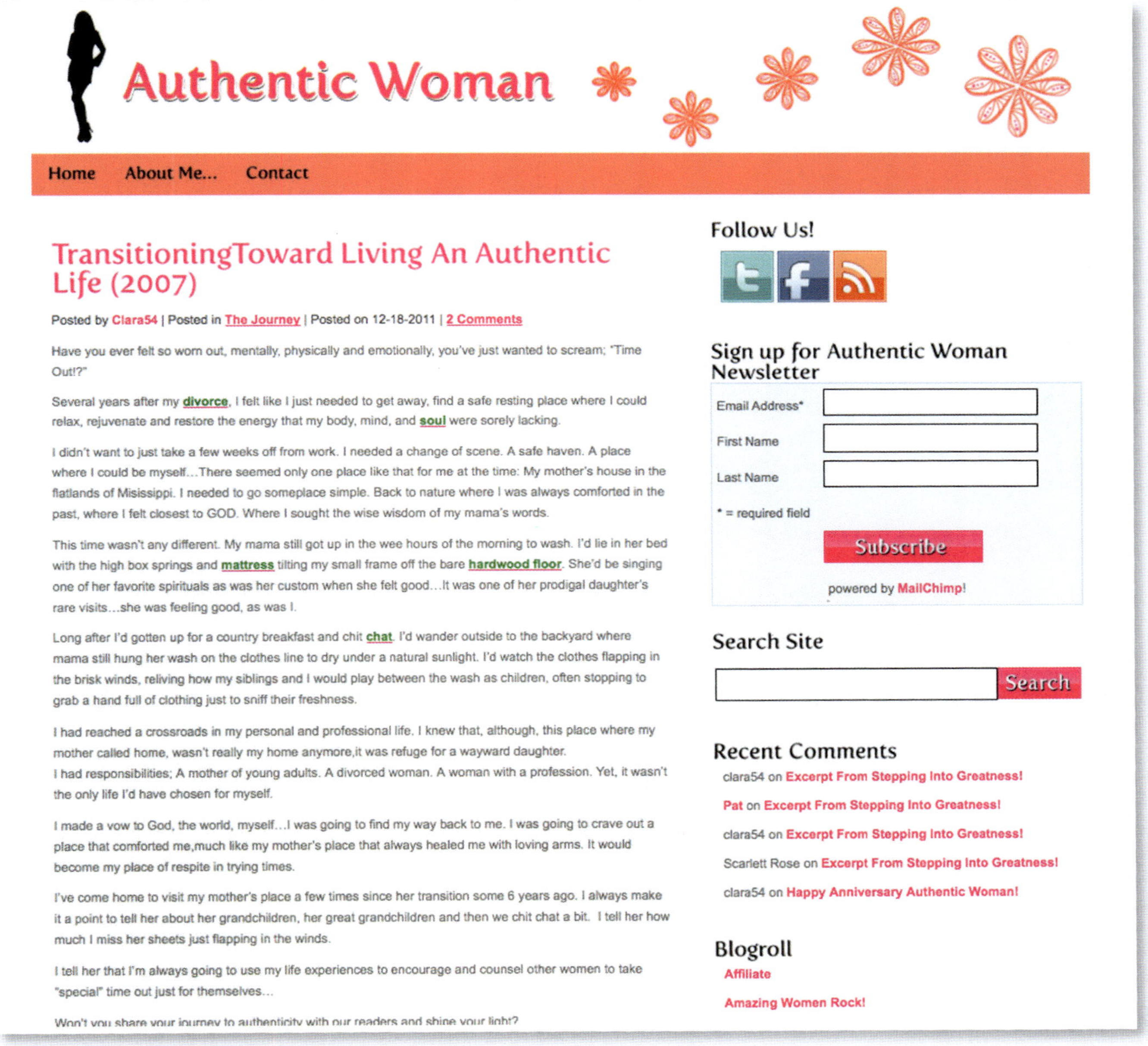

Authentic Woman

Home About Me... Contact

TransitioningToward Living An Authentic Life (2007)

Posted by Clara54 | Posted in The Journey | Posted on 12-18-2011 | 2 Comments

Have you ever felt so worn out, mentally, physically and emotionally, you've just wanted to scream; "Time Out!?"

Several years after my divorce, I felt like I just needed to get away, find a safe resting place where I could relax, rejuvenate and restore the energy that my body, mind, and soul were sorely lacking.

I didn't want to just take a few weeks off from work. I needed a change of scene. A safe haven. A place where I could be myself…There seemed only one place like that for me at the time: My mother's house in the flatlands of Mississippi. I needed to go someplace simple. Back to nature where I was always comforted in the past, where I felt closest to GOD. Where I sought the wise wisdom of my mama's words.

This time wasn't any different. My mama still got up in the wee hours of the morning to wash. I'd lie in her bed with the high box springs and mattress tilting my small frame off the bare hardwood floor. She'd be singing one of her favorite spirituals as was her custom when she felt good…It was one of her prodigal daughter's rare visits…she was feeling good, as was I.

Long after I'd gotten up for a country breakfast and chit chat, I'd wander outside to the backyard where mama still hung her wash on the clothes line to dry under a natural sunlight. I'd watch the clothes flapping in the brisk winds, reliving how my siblings and I would play between the wash as children, often stopping to grab a hand full of clothing just to sniff their freshness.

I had reached a crossroads in my personal and professional life. I knew that, although, this place where my mother called home, wasn't really my home anymore,it was refuge for a wayward daughter.
I had responsibilities; A mother of young adults. A divorced woman. A woman with a profession. Yet, it wasn't the only life I'd have chosen for myself.

I made a vow to God, the world, myself…I was going to find my way back to me. I was going to crave out a place that comforted me,much like my mother's place that always healed me with loving arms. It would become my place of respite in trying times.

I've come home to visit my mother's place a few times since her transition some 6 years ago. I always make it a point to tell her about her grandchildren, her great grandchildren and then we chit chat a bit. I tell her how much I miss her sheets just flapping in the winds.

I tell her that I'm always going to use my life experiences to encourage and counsel other women to take "special" time out just for themselves…

Won't you share your journey to authenticity with our readers and shine your light?

Follow Us!

Sign up for Authentic Woman Newsletter

Email Address*

First Name

Last Name

* = required field

Subscribe

powered by MailChimp!

Search Site

Search

Recent Comments

clara54 on Excerpt From Stepping Into Greatness!

Pat on Excerpt From Stepping Into Greatness!

clara54 on Excerpt From Stepping Into Greatness!

Scarlett Rose on Excerpt From Stepping Into Greatness!

clara54 on Happy Anniversary Authentic Woman!

Blogroll

Affiliate

Amazing Women Rock!

#6 INSPIRATIONAL

People love stories and quotes that make them feel warm and fuzzy all over. Your audience is no different. You can share how someone accomplished a goal, overcame an obstacle, or performed a small deed with great results. These posts can be profiles, interviews, inspirational quotes, or positive affirmations.

Pro:

- It's always a great feeling to help other people

Other Considerations:

- You'll have more stories than you'll have time to share
- Encourage your readers to write and submit their stories on the condition that entries with the fewest editorial needs will be posted

SAMPLE INSPIRATIONAL POST

Vikram Roy's Blog is full of positive energy that flows from the spirit of its creator. The post below highlights great people that are committed to world peace. This site is proof that your audience is attracted to you and the value you provide.

What's the point? Just be you.

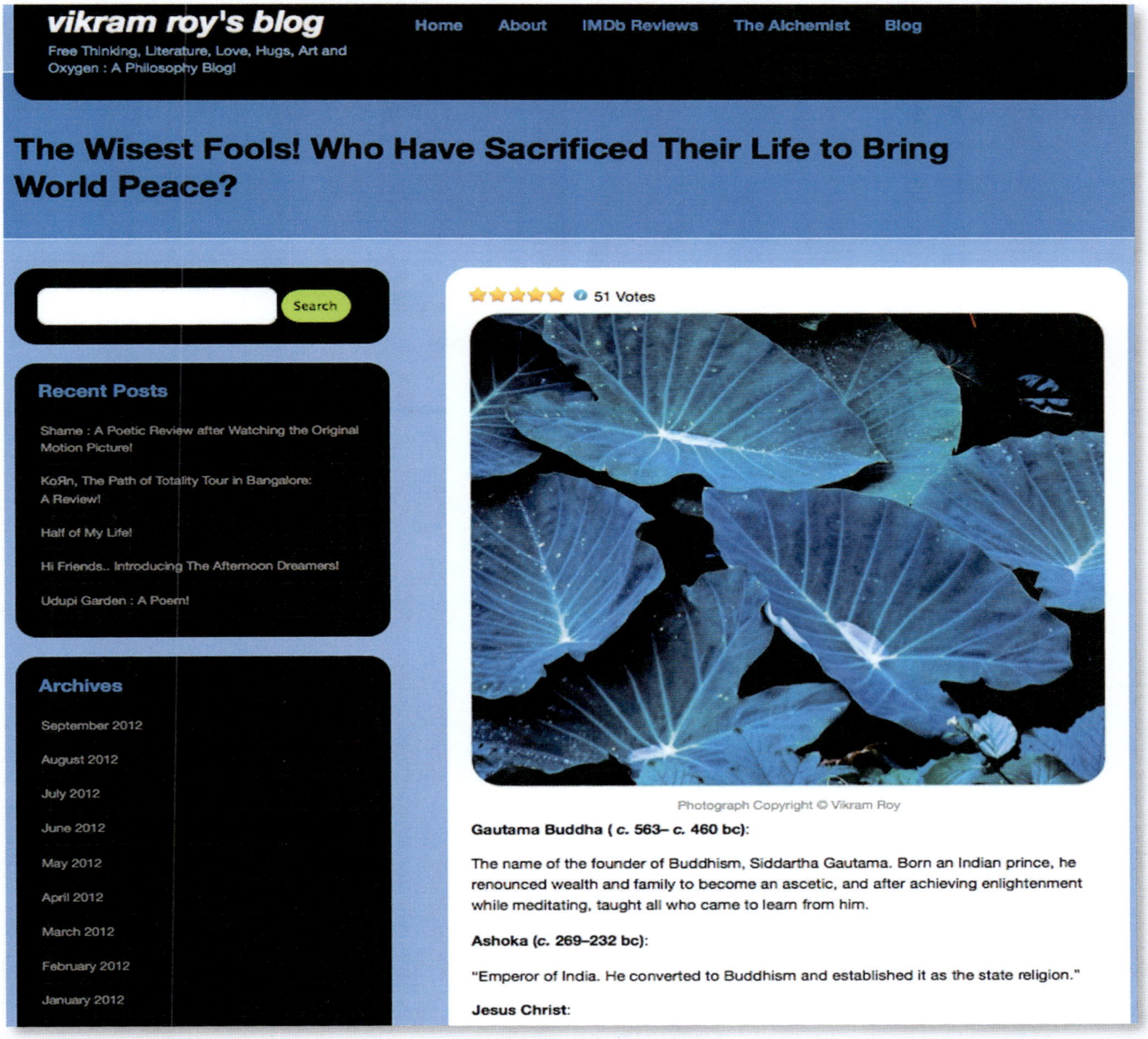

#7 RESEARCH

A research post can be an in-depth informational article, some type of review, or a comparison post where you share extensive details about what something is, how it works, and how it can benefit your audience.

There are three ways to incorporate research on your site:

1. Provide a step-by-step guide on how you are researching a topic
2. Highlight findings from a research project you are working on
3. Create a research site just for a topic in which you are interested

Pros:

- You can introduce new topics to your audience
- Your site can serve as a journal of your research project, which you can use to track your progress

Other Considerations:

- Conducting research is time-consuming and very tedious
- You may have to make boring topics more engaging
- Your audience might become interested in a particular topic because of your passion

SAMPLE RESEARCH POST

My site, Real Skate Stories, was created to collect roller skating memories of people who are or were quad skaters. Visitors can type in their stories, leave audio or video comments, and upload images. My goal is to amass the largest online database of oral roller skating history as told by the people who lived it.

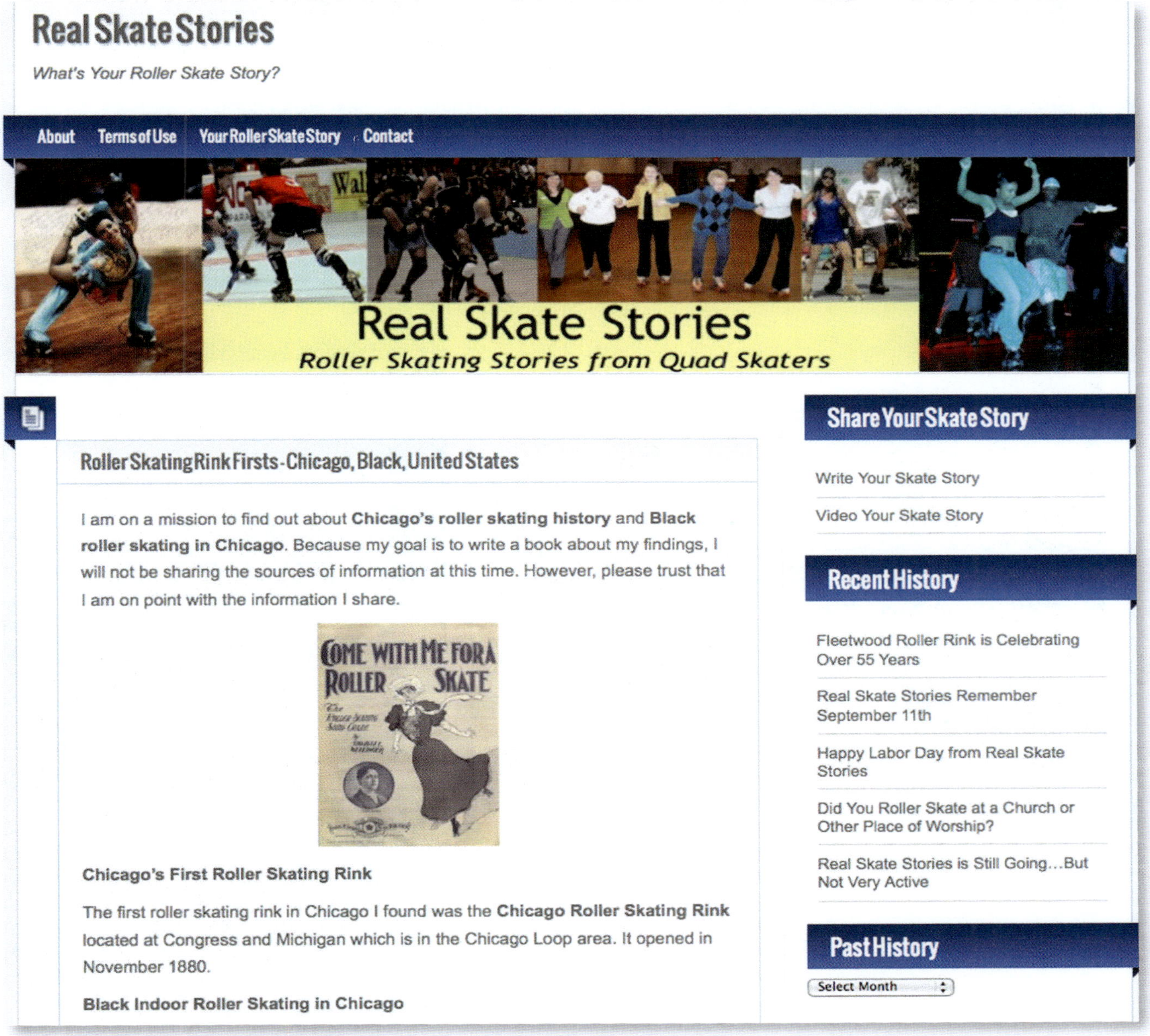

#8 LISTS

Lists are articles where bullet points or numbers are used to separate points. They can be how-to, informational, or "the best of" posts. These posts can be as short as two points or as long as 100 points, depending on the topic.

Pro:

- List posts are perfect for when you need a "right quick" post because they are easy for you to write and easy for your audience to follow

Other Consideration:

- Resist the temptation to write list posts only. Boost your creative flow and audience engagement by mixing up the type of content and media tools used to share information

SAMPLE LIST POST

The following numbered list post on John Chow's site shares things that you can do to take your blog to the next level personally, professionally, and financially. Some tips will be quick to implement while others may take more time.

#9 CHECKLISTS

According to Karol K. of Online Business Design, checklists are specific tasks that should be performed to complete a project. A traditional checklist is a PDF form that has empty boxes that should be checked to show that a particular step has been completed. She also advises to "...write a post describing what it's for and how to use it."

Regardless of whether the checklist you're writing is telling the reader how to do something or about items they should have, make sure that all the steps are listed.

Pro:

- Providing very specific steps on how to complete a task will make peoples' lives easier

Other Considerations:

- Make sure the checklist can be downloaded and printed
- Be as accurate as possible. A missed step could confuse the user

SAMPLE CHECKLIST POST

Daniel Scocco shared a very thorough checklist post on Daily Blog Tips. He included a list in the post, provided an explanation of each step, and made it downloadable as a PDF.

#10 LINK POSTS

Link posts are similar to list posts except there is an actual link to internal or external content. Internal linking, or deep linking, occurs when you link to previously written stories on your site. This keeps older content relevant and increases your site's placement on search engines. Linking to other sites is called external linking.

Pros:

- These posts are quick and easy to create
- You can give exposure to other bloggers by linking to relevant content on their sites

Other Considerations:

- Be sure you are linking to relevant content and credible sites
- You won't always get links back from the sites to which you have linked
- Linking to bad sites diminishes the credibility of your site
- Getting external links from reputable sites strengthens the popularity and search engine rankings of your blog

SAMPLE LINK POST

Keisha Easley, the owner of We Blog Better, put extra time, effort, and creativity into this link post. Instead of linking to text, she linked to screenshots. Do you see any familiar sites in the post below?

TESTIMONIALS

Marcie Hill is all write. In her latest book, "62 Posts to Overcome Blogger's Block," the generous and prolific writer, author and trainer does her best to clean up the blogosphere by giving helpful and critical instructions to bloggers who dare to have deeper impact and better content by moving past the blocks to meaningful posts. With solid advice, anecdotes and best-practice testimonials, Ms. Hill is able to deliver a course in blogging useful to any individual, corporation, nonprofit, institution or brand hoping to augment readership, audience involvement and effectiveness. If only every blogger heeded her advice, then the world would be freed from irrelevant postings and tedious, chronological regurgitations of a life. No matter how you use the web, you can use this book to improve your digital communication. This needs to be in the library of every journalist, blogger, communications director and social media expert. Read, go forth and blog richly!

Michele Weldon - author, journalist, assistant professor of journalism at The Medill School, Northwestern University and seminar leader at The OpEd Project.

PART 2

MULTIMEDIA POSTS

Multimedia posts are "fun" posts where imagery and visualization trumps the written word. Although these posts are a great way to diversify your content and engage your readers, they are time consuming to create and editing can eat up loads of time depending on your editing skill level and the type of media you use. It is also important to make sure that your hosting site has ample storage space for multimedia files because they tend to be huge.

If you are "borrowing" other people's creative works, be sure to ask for permission or give them credit for their intellectual property. All written and visual works are copyrighted as soon as they are created whether or not the person's name is on the work. Check Creative Commons to find images, music, and video files that artists have given the public certain rights to use. Keep in mind that paying someone to create or edit these files can be pretty pricey.

There are nine types of posts that fall into this category:

1. **Photos**
2. **Videos**
3. **Audio**
4. **Presentations**
5. **Screencasts**
6. **Infographics**
7. **Animation**
8. **Teleseminars**
9. **Webinars**

#11 PHOTOS

There are three ways photos can be used on your site:

1. To accompany written stories
2. To create a photoblog, which is an entire blog with photos only
3. To create a post where a photo is the message

Photos that accompany written stories are more common on sites because they add more impact to the story's message. Photoblogs are growing in popularity among photographers of all skill levels. Then there are times when a picture is the message and no words are needed.

You can download images found on search engines for free, but this is a very common method that is used by many bloggers and content creators. Using some of these images could violate copyright laws because you are stealing someone else's intellectual property. To avoid possible legal action, find sites that offer royalty free images or purchase images from stock photography sites.

Here are five of the most popular sites from which you can obtain images:

- Creative Commons
- Pinterest
- Getty Images
- Dreamstime
- iStockphoto

The best option, however, is to take and use your own photos using a camera, a webcam, or a mobile phone. This alleviates any copyright issues because you own and control everything.

Pros:

- Some images have powerful messages
- You have plenty of photos options and even more sources from which to obtain images

Other Considerations:

- Be mindful about stealing other people's work. All original works are copyrighted as soon as they are created whether or not the creator's name or logo is on the image
- When you borrow from other people, be sure to give them credit
- Try to get permission to use photos prior to posting them
- Use images that are relevant to the topic of discussion
- When you use downloaded images or stock photography, you will see them often on different sites because everyone has access to them, so try to capture and use original images

SAMPLE PHOTOBLOG

Peggy Stevenson, better known as B.C., posts a new image every day on Chicago: A Daily Photo Blog. As you can see, some of her individual images tell powerful stories without words.

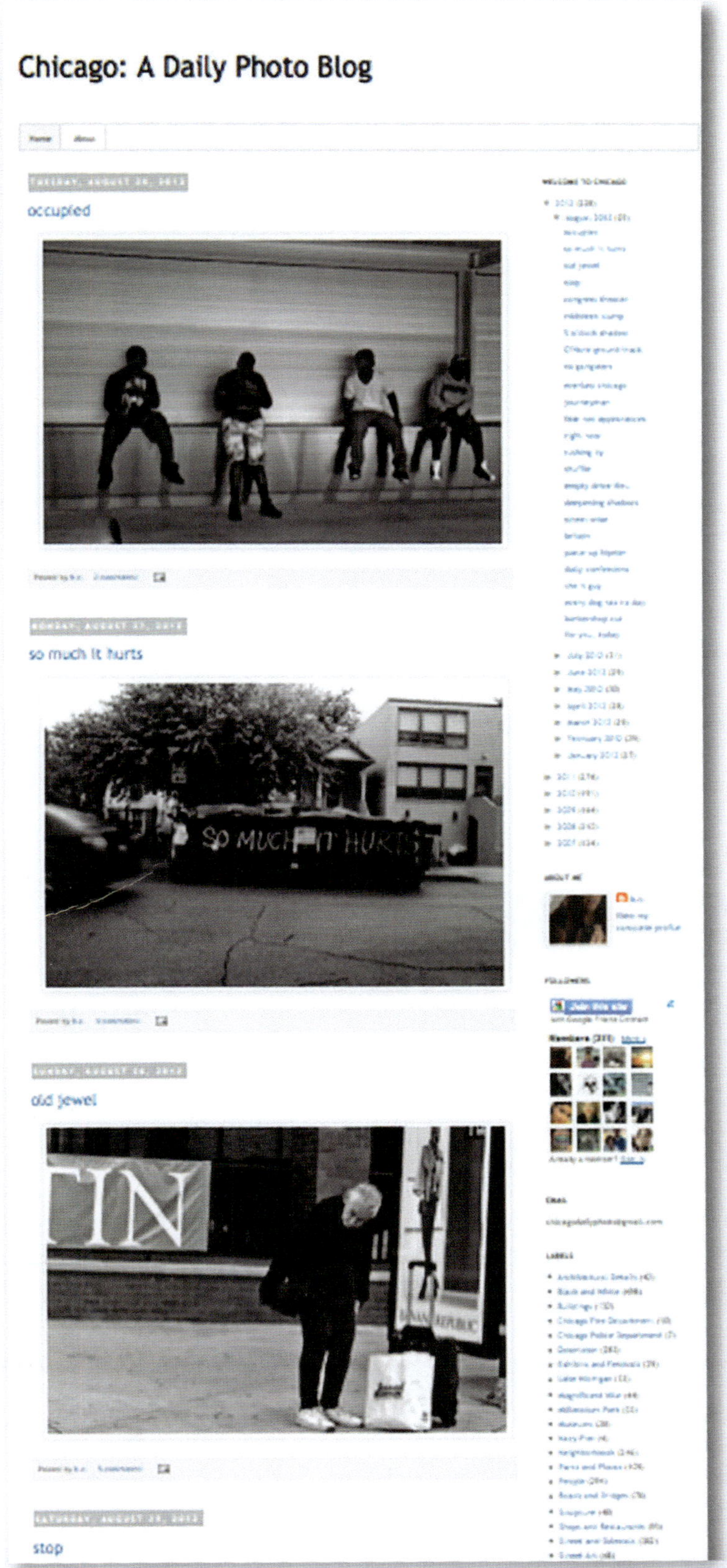

#12 VIDEOS

Video blogs (vlogs) are becoming even more popular than photoblogs. When your audience can see you, they feel like they know you and this helps to develop a more immediate rapport. In fact, research shows that e-mails with video are opened more often than text-only messages.

Like photos, there are several ways to use videos on your site. They can be borrowed or created; and they do not always have to be related to your blog topics. It's okay to have a little fun by veering from your usual topics.

Videos can be produced with a webcam, a camcorder, a pocket camcorder, or a mobile phone. They can also be created and recorded online with Skype, Oovoo, and Google+ Hangouts. Also, there are tons of mobile apps you can use to record and upload videos directly to your blog.

There are five ways to create videos for your site:

- Produce a talking head video by recording yourself speaking
- Interview someone or record conversations
- Record events taking place or people in action
- Record Skype calls with Vodburner or Supertintin
- Record a Google+ Hangout

You can upload and download from videos from several sites, including:

YouTube vimeo viddler

Pros:

- You can connect with your online audience faster, especially if the videos are captivating
- It is easier to record your story than to write content
- You have several options to record and obtain videos

Other Considerations:

- Make sure your video has a purpose and is relevant to your message
- Make sure you and your guest have a good online presence, which includes a pleasing personality, vocal variety, and limited physical and verbal distracters
- Be sure to have good sound and image quality
- Get your interviewee's permission to record prior to interviewing and recording because unauthorized recording is illegal in some states
- To upload video directly to your site may require a little technical knowledge, which could cause frustration for technically challenged bloggers and content creators
- If someone tells you they are not video-ready, believe him or her

SAMPLE VIDEOBLOG

Gary Vaynerchuk became an international wine connoisseur and video sensation with his video blog, Wine Library TV (WLTV). It all began with his concern about the lack of education in the wine industry. Instead of complaining, he reached into his knowledge banks and created WLTV to share tips and resources on all things wine. Lesson from Gary: being a solution to problems pays – literally and figuratively.

#13 AUDIO

You can add audio to a blog post or create an audio blog, also known as a podcast, by producing the audio recording yourself or downloading it from other sources.

There are four ways to produce audio:

1. Record yourself speaking
2. Interview someone or record conversations (legally)
3. Audio record Skype calls
4. Use the audio from video-recorded materials

Following are five ways to audio record content for your site:

- Digital voice recorder
- Online audio recorders
- Teleconferencing programs
- Mobile apps
- Dragon Naturally Speaking

Pros:

- It is easier to speak your content than to write it
- There are several audio recording options, as well as programs that turn audio into text
- Your audience can perform other tasks while listening to your audio

Other Considerations:

- People can hear your enthusiasm and energy, so put your best self forward
- Face it, some people are just not pleasing to the ear. They may have annoying voices, speak in a monotone manner, or simply say too many "ums" and '"ahs". In these situations, you may need to write the interview or become an expert at audio editing
- Posting audio requires a little technical knowledge
- Try to filter background noises and other distractions when recording
- If borrowing audio files, be sure to respect copyright laws and give credit when it's due
- Editing may consume a lot of time, even with short recordings
- Get permission to audio record the interviewee prior to the interview. Like video, unauthorized audio recording is illegal in some states

SAMPLE AUDIO POST

Mitch Mitchell gives his audience two options to receive his message: text and audio. Audio is great for people who would rather listen to content instead of reading or watching it.

#14 PRESENTATIONS

Presentations allow you to combine your audio, video, photos, and writings to create a multimedia experience for your audience.

You can create photo slideshows, videos, and PowerPoint or Prezi presentations. Presentations can also be uploaded and downloaded from SlideShare, Scribd, and other presentation-sharing sites.

Pros:

- Presentations help build your credibility as an authority
- You will boost your multimedia production and editing skills
- You will have fun creating and sharing your unique presentations

Other Considerations:

- Do not use too many images and words on individual slides
- Make your presentation pleasing to the eyes with relevant designs, colors, and images
- Be sure that the information presented is relevant and organized
- Creating presentations can be time consuming
- Poor quality videos, images, and audio can distract from your project
- Respect copyright laws when using other people's work
- Advance planning can make creating your presentation easier and more time efficient

SAMPLE POST WITH PRESENTATION

In this post, Liz Strauss enhanced her message by embedding a SlideShare presentation. She benefited three ways from doing this. First, her expert status increased with her blog audience. Second, her site moved up the ranks on search engines. Third, she gained more visibility on SlideShare.

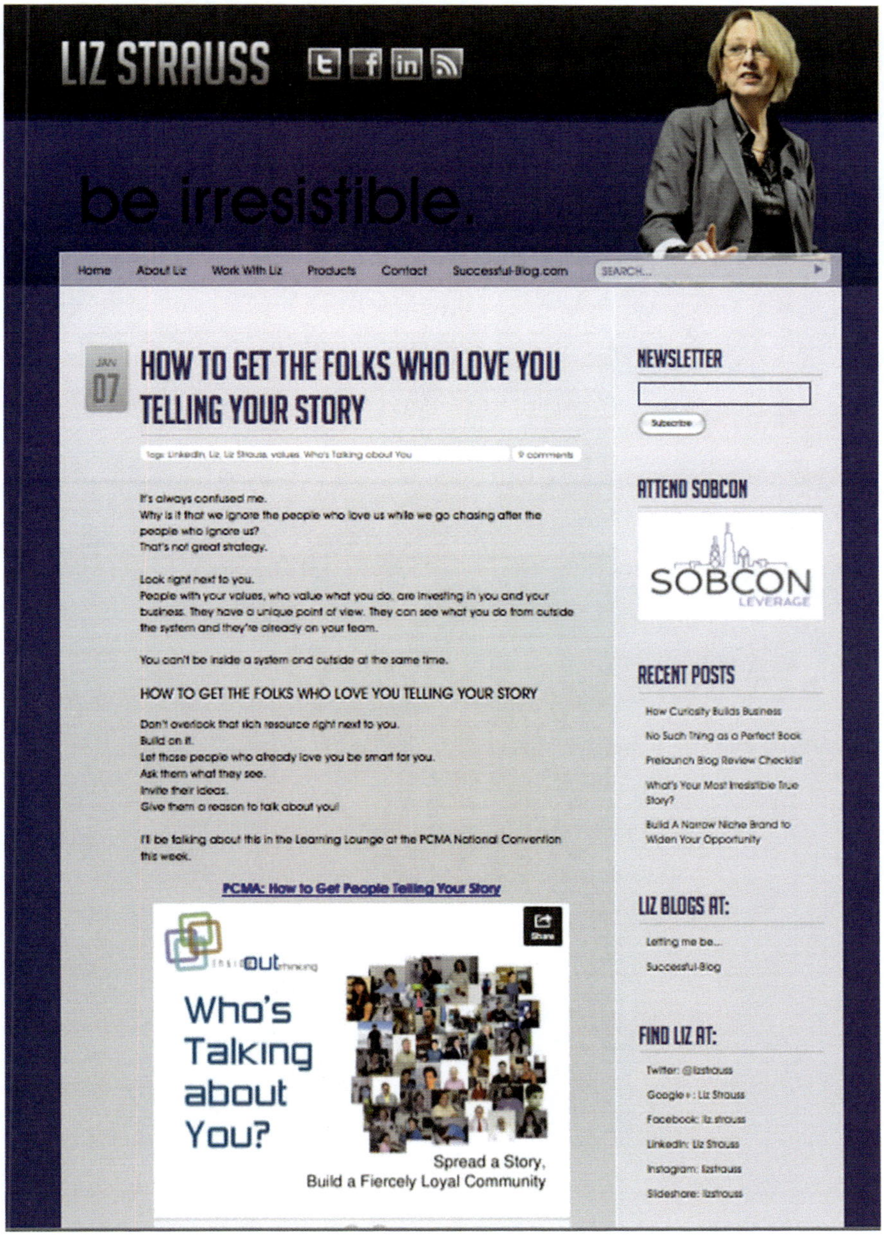

#15 SCREENCASTS

Screencasts allow you to record everything that's happening on your screen. They are used mostly for video tutorials and can be created with free or paid software. Most paid software has free offerings with limited options, which is sufficient for smaller projects.

For a comprehensive listing of the different types of screencasting software and how to use the software effectively, check out *The Screencasting Handbook* by Ian Ozsvald. In the meantime, try these three free programs to get started:

- Screencast-o-matic
- Jing
- Camstudio

Pros:

- Free screencasting software can help get you started
- You can build credibility in your niche as a topic expert and multimedia guru

Other Considerations:

- Free software has limitations, so consider investing if you plan to use screencasts regularly
- Make sure your content is clear and organized
- Good sound and image quality, as well as diction, are essential
- Speak clearly with vocal variety and exude personality
- Most screencasting programs give you the option to upload videos directly to YouTube. This will help to expand your platform and boost your search engine ranking

SAMPLE POST WITH SCREENCAST

Chris Brogan got a four-for-one audience visibility deal with a screencast he created on how to use Google+. First, he retrieved content from his *Google+ for Business* book. Second, he uploaded the screencast to YouTube, which is owned by Google. Third, he posted it on his site. Lastly, his name and site ranking shot through the roof on search engines.

This screencast was a great way for Chris to sell books, boost his online visibility, and increase his authority as a Google+ guru.

#16 INFOGRAPHICS

Infographics are used to share data visually. They turn boring statistics and data into visually pleasing charts, graphics, and timelines that are easy to read and comprehend.

In addition to researching topics, infographic creators write information down so they can see what they want to share. Then they graphically create this data so **you can see what they want to say**.

Following are three sites where you can create different types of infographics for free:

- Easel.ly
- Infogr.am
- Picktochart

Pros:

- Infographics are very engaging and fun to read
- They englighten people by helping them see the information you're sharing

Other Considerations:

- Infographics are time consuming and can be expensive to create
- If someone else is creating images for you, they may not be able to express your message in the way you'd want it expressed

SAMPLE INFOGRAPHIC SITE

Daily Infographic, created by Jay Willingham, is chock full of infographics created by visual designers with a variety of talents and interests.

#17 ANIMATION

Animation is one of the most overlooked additions to blog posts. Who really thinks, "Oh, let me find or create an animation to post today?" You may not find many of these posts unless animation is your career or hobby, or if you happen to run across one that fits your blog's topic. Animation will definitely add personality to your site and topics.

Mashable, the online technology and social media authority, shared the following animation creation programs:

- GoAnimate
- Dvolver
- Animoto

Pros:

- Animation adds a different flavor to your posts
- It will capture the attention of people who don't ordinarily visit your site
- There are free software programs that allow you to create your own animations

Other Considerations:

- Animation is very time consuming to create and could be expensive if you pay someone to create it for you
- Respect copyright laws when using the works of others

SAMPLE ANIMATION BLOG

Animator Martin Lindsey shares his creative talents with the world by posting his works on his site, The Animated World of Martin Lindsey, and on YouTube.

#18 TELESEMINARS

Bloggers are increasingly using teleseminars to expand their offline platform. Teleseminars are seminars where people call in or click a link to listen to a person speak on a topic. Sometimes the presenter allows the listeners to ask questions.

In a teleseminar, you can expound on topics on your site or introduce new ones. The presentation can be audio or video recorded and then either e-mailed to your audience or embedded on your site.

The more popular teleseminar or teleconferencing programs are:

- Instant Teleseminar
- Free Conference Calling
- GotoMeeting

Pros:

- Teleseminars help build your platform, expertise, and e-mail list
- Your online relationships can become offline opportunities

Other Considerations:

- You must market your teleseminar, which can be challenging even with social media
- Consistent marketing is required to increase the visibility of your teleseminars and to grow your audience
- You must sound confident and welcoming during your presentation; otherwise, you may lose your audience during the call
- Write out your presentation prior to the event and practice your delivery often
- Your audience must feel your passion and excitement; otherwise, they will hang up
- Allow people to ask questions if time permits
- Prepare for technical glitches

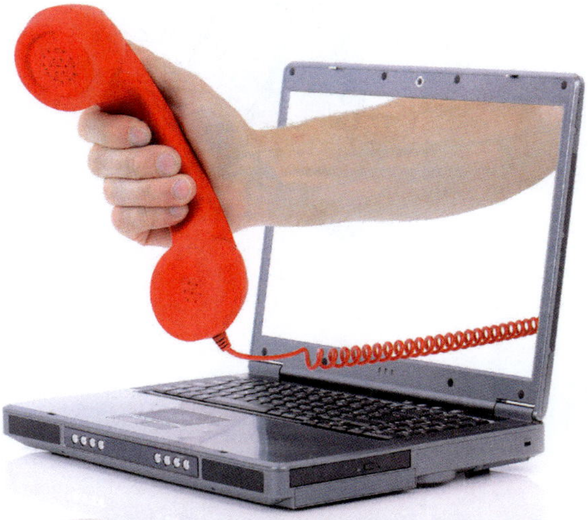

SAMPLE POST WITH TELESEMINAR

Electra Ford, the creator of Virtual Office Center, embedded an audio recording of her teleseminar and added the transcript to her site. This enabled her to distribute her content through audio, visual, and written channels on the web.

#19 WEBINARS

Webinars, or web-based seminars, are conferences conducted over the web with two or more parties. Offered by third party providers, webinars are used for trainings, lectures, meetings, and short presentations.

They are usually conducted offline and then embedded into your site. Webinars can be presentations, audio, or video. Like teleseminars, you can present topics from your site or introduce new ones.

Three webinar software programs to consider include:

- Anymeeting
- WebEx
- Skype

Pros:

- There are companies that offer usage of free software for a limited time
- This is a way to grow your online and offline audiences and boost your authority on your topics

Other Considerations:

- Keep the limitations of free software programs in mind, and consider investing if you conduct webinars frequently
- Be sure the information is clear and flows smoothly
- From your personality to word choice to how you speak, your presentation must sparkle
- Be aware of technical challenges that may arise

SAMPLE WEBINAR IN POST

As shown on her site, Denise Wakeman is committed to helping clients boost their visibility on the web. She did a great job of increasing her own visibility with the webinar replay she posted on her site.

By making her webinar available to her audience members who could not attend the actual event, she was viewed more favorably by her followers. Second, she was able to promote the expertise of Kathleen Gage, the webinar presenter. Third, she had ready-made content for her site, so she was able to take a break from her regular posting schedule.

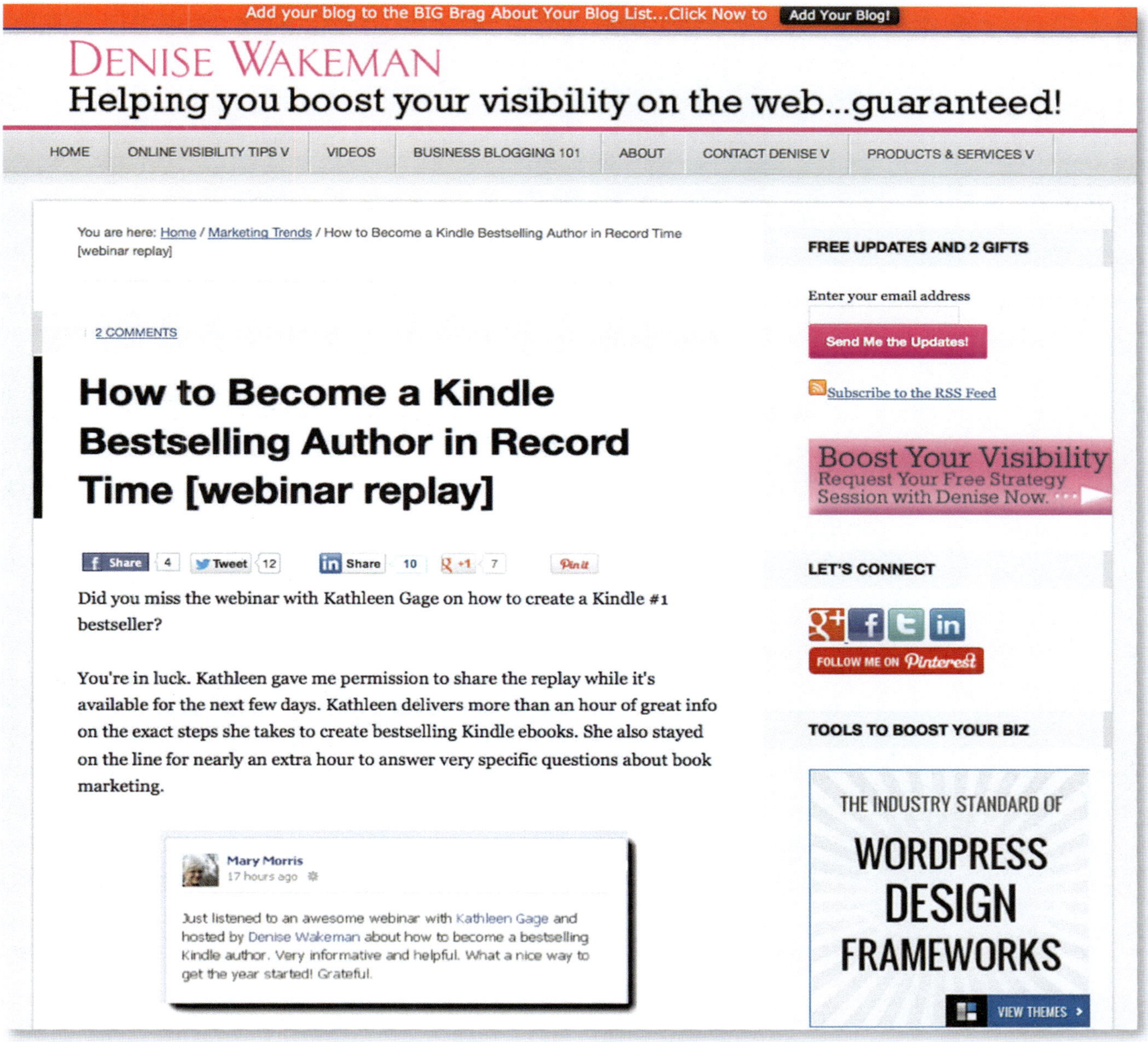

PART 3

HONOR OTHERS

Some of the greatest posts you can create are those in which you honor others. Spotlight someone you admire; a person who has impacted your life; or someone who is up-and-coming in his or her career. The options are unlimited. The upside to creating these posts is that everyone wins. It will do your heart well to produce it; your honoree will feel special; and you will make an emotional connection with your audience.

These posts can be in written, audio, video, photo, or presentation formats. If your creativity is in overdrive, consider creating animations and infographics.

There are ten ways you can honor others on your site:

1. **Profiles**
2. **Interviews**
3. **Guest Posts**
4. **Testimonials**
5. **What Others Are Saying**
6. **Someone You Admire**
7. **Charity/Causes**
8. **Comments of Readers**
9. **Gratitude/Thank you**
10. **Boast Posts**

#20 PROFILES

Research a person you admire and then write about him or her. It could be someone you feel **is** interesting; someone who is doing something interesting; or someone who has done something newsworthy. Highlight things that matter to your audience. How did they get to where they are now? What challenges did they overcome? Who helped them or whom did they help along the way?

These articles can be written in first or third person, and can be audio or video recorded. Ultimately, you want your audience to feel an emotional connection to your honoree. Be sure to attach a photo to add an extra "oomph" to your story.

Pros:

- You can honor who you want, when you want, and how you want
- Show your love for your readers by sharing their profiles

Other Considerations:

- Be sure to plan prior to beginning the project
- It takes time to conduct research and to schedule interviews
- Try to get your honoree's untold stories and experiences
- Keep in mind that if something is not interesting to you, it won't appeal to your audience either

SAMPLE PROFILE SITE

Women Worth Watching, created by Diversity Journal, is a site that profiles female executives and the organizations in which they work. They even engage audience members by extending the opportunity to nominate women executives they admire.

#21 INTERVIEWS

An interview occurs when one person gets information from another person either in written, audio or video formats.

Interviews are an excellent way to:

- Give exposure to people who are just starting out
- Speak with experts in your industry
- Talk to someone "just because"
- Provide a platform to share unheard voices, thoughts, and opinions

Pros:

- This is a win-win for traffic generation when both the interviewee and interviewer post the interview on their sites and promote it on their social networks
- Your interviews could be the beginning of a podcast, a videoblog (vlog) series, or an Internet TV show
- You will get great information as well as different perspectives and experiences

Other Considerations:

- The energy of the interviewer, the personality of the interviewee, and the responses to the questions asked contribute to the success of the interview
- Try to prepare for interviews as much as possible beforehand
- Be creative by making boring topics more engaging
- Be mindful of interviewees that speak in a monotone manner, have annoying voices, or lack personality when recording
- When writing interviews, try to keep them short and engaging. It's hard to read online, and it's even harder to keep your audience's attention
- Maintain control of the interview by keeping your interviewee on topic when the discussion goes in an unexpected direction or when your interviewee gets emotional

SAMPLE INTERVIEW

Jennifer Brown Banks shared an interview with Hope Clark, the Creator of Funds for Writers, on her writing site, Pen & Prosper. Because of Jennifer's style of writing, the questions she asked, and the image she added, her readers were able to personally connect with Hope.

0 More ▾ Next Blog»

Pen & Pro$per

...KNOW MORE. GROW MORE. "REQUIRED READING" FOR TODAY'S SMART WRITER...

Testimonials ...This Gun's for Hire. | Write For Us | My Guest Posts | About | Contact | The "Buzz" ...What Readers Say

Monday, February 6, 2012

A Glimpse of Hope-Pen & Prosper Presents Hope Clark of Funds for Writers

For more than a decade, Hope Clark has been "showing writers the money!"
She is the creator and editor of Funds for Writers, an accomplished writer and author. Today, Pen and Prosper provides readers with a two-part post on the woman behind the words and the secrets to her success.

1.Can you tell us a little about who you are and your background?

That's a book! It would be for anyone. The short version is that I am editor of FundsforWriters.com and a mystery novelist. My first mystery in the Carolina Slade Mystery Series is Lowcountry Bribe, coming out from Bell Bridge Books (www.bellbridgebooks.com) in February 2012 – available at all book stores in brick or online. FundsforWriters.com is a website, four newsletters and a general world of writing resources for writers struggling to earn a living doing what they love. Writer's Digest selected FundsforWriters for its 101 Best Websites for Writers for the last eleven years, and it's being considered for 2012.

My education is a BS in Agriculture, and I have 25 years under my belt working for the US Department of Agriculture in rural development. That non-writing background might seem to

PROBLOGGER

As seen on Pro Blogger, Men With Pens, Daily Blog Tips, Technorati, WritetoDone, The Well-Fed Writer, and other popular sites...

About Me

Jennifer Brown Banks
Illinois, United States

I'm a professional, veteran freelance writer, columnist, Pro Blogger, and "Ghost" writer with about 600 publishing credits, both online and in print publications, in multiple genres. My work has appeared at popular, award-winning sites and magazines such as: Pro

#22 GUEST POSTS

Guest posts are win-wins for the blog owner and the guest blogger. As the guest blogger, you are expanding your reach by sharing your stories, experiences, and lessons with a different audience. You are also giving the site owner a break, which is always appreciated. Also, the audience of the hosting blog gets to hear different voices and perspectives.

Pros:

- The blog owner gets a break with guest posts
- Guest bloggers can step outside their comfort zones by writing on different topics in different styles

Other Considerations:

- Some people have good intentions, but poor writing skills
- Read a few posts on the site of interest before pitching story ideas to improve the chances of your post being accepted

SAMPLE POST ABOUT GUEST POSTS

Gail Gardner, the creator of GrowMap, wrote a comprehensive post on how to guest blog on her site. She also provided tips on how to get your guest posts accepted on other sites, as well as samples of her submissions.

#23 TESTIMONIALS

Anytime someone says something positive about how you impacted his or her life in any way, make it a blog post. Testimonials are the best evidence of the value you provide personally and professionally. They can be written, audio or video recorded. You can also copy and paste status updates from your social sites.

Pros:

- Testimonials are the greatest proof of the value you add to the lives of others
- Oftentimes, they come unexpectedly

Other Considerations:

- Make sure the testimonials are from credible sources
- Do not be afraid to share your testimonials as blog posts
- Don't write a testimonial for someone else just because they wrote one for you; do it because you want to

SAMPLE POST ABOUT TESTIMONIALS

Social@BloggingTracker's owner, Ching Ya, wrote an extremely comprehensive post on how to add client testimonials to your site. Specifically, she provided:

1. Descriptions of the tools you can use to add testimonials
2. Visual examples of each tool
3. A brief lesson on how to use them

#24 WHAT OTHERS ARE SAYING

There are three ways to create a What Others Are Saying post:

1. Take a statement from someone else's site and contribute your thoughts and opinions
2. Make a statement and add links from other sites to support it
3. Respectfully respond to the criticism and negative comments of others

Pros:

- Sharing your thoughts can increase your status as an expert or resource
- By linking to other sites, you can increase your online visibility

Other Considerations:

- Be selective about whom and what you repeat
- Do not criticize the person; focus on the issue
- People may get offended by what you say. Use this as a public relations or customer service opportunity
- Give credit where credit is due

SAMPLE WHAT OTHERS ARE SAYING POST

Jayme Soulati wrote the ideal What Others Are Saying post. She began by responding to a comment someone made on her blog; she gave the person credit. She then referred to a post on another site, and then shared her opinion on the topic.

Should Health Of Blog Community Align To ROI?

Jayme Soulati | 01/11/2012 | 42 Comments

I had a post all ready for today, and then @TheJackB spat all over my blog in comments. I could not let that slide, so this post is a compilation of his musings and mine. (You get co-authorship, TheJack, but just not in the byline…heh.)

The Sales Lion wrote a post yesterday about why community is not Holy Grail of blogging that I'm sure is creating a slew of comments, not the most of which is Gini Dietrich (although I've not been over to comment myself). Marcus said something to the effect that "Gini shocked the blogosphere admitting her business almost went bankrupt in 2011 in spite of her healthy blog, Spin Sucks, and its huge community with lengthier commentary." (paraphrase)

IMHO (In my humble opinion), Arment Dietrich is a service firm; it delivers professional services and seeks clients to pay it to stay viable. Gini is the point person, face, poster child, CEO, founder, biz dev artist for her firm, and, oh, yeah, she's chief cook and bottle writer for her highly popularly ranked and accoladed blog, Spin Sucks. Her new product, Spin Sucks Pro, for which peeps will subscribe to content and teachings via webinars and writings from around the 'sphere, launches soon (after a one-year delay during which she had to fire a tech team and start from scratch). (Never write sentences like these two.)

When you're running a successful digital marketing/PR shop with staff and expensive headquarters near the Merchandise Mart in Chicago, and you're launching a brand new online moneymaker that fails and requires an immediate new investment in tech dollars and clients refuse to pay you for six months and the economy sucks (like Spin), then what's so surprising about a firm nearly going belly up (in spite of a successful blog and community)?

This dilemma is one many successful entrepreneurs face – how to clone oneself. We are the brand and brain power clients wants, hire and require. Using Gini Dietrich was a poor example to showcase that a

#25 SOMEONE YOU ADMIRE

You can write a post or create an entire site around someone you admire. It could be a friend, family member, celebrity, or other role model.

Pros:

- One of the best ways to honor someone and enhance your relationship with that person is to share why you admire or appreciate him or her
- Encourage your audience to share their admiration for others
- Be sure to spotlight your readers

Other Considerations:

- You may get tired of writing about one person, so diversify your subjects
- If you have featured several people you admire, find common themes and create a book, slideshow, or other product for your site
- Utilize multimedia tools to share your story

SAMPLE SOMEONE YOU ADMIRE BLOG

Aminah Hanan dedicated an entire site to First Lady Michelle Obama. Started in 2008, she has successfully countered mainstream media attacks on the First Lady. She has managed to keep the focus on the person instead of distractors like stereotypes, racial and gender biases, or other -isms that arose.

#26 CHARITY/CAUSE

There are three ways to promote your favorite charity or cause on your site:

1. Create a site specifically for your favorite cause or charity
2. Collect donations for specific charities
3. Educate your audience on a particular cause, including the background of the issue, what's being done to correct it, prevention tips, and available resources

Pros:

- It's a win-win for you and the cause or charity you're supporting. By giving exposure to the organization in need, you are increasing your credibility as a resource
- Your audience may rally around the cause with you
- You are educating your audience on topics and resources that they previously may not have been aware of

Other Considerations:

- You may get a flood of requests to support other causes and charities
- If you're collecting donations, don't let your messages end after the funds have been collected; continue to educate and update your audiences
- Build your readers' trust so they feel confident enough to send donations
- You may become a spokesperson for that cause

SAMPLE CAUSE SITE

The Red Pump Project is Lovette "Luvvie" Ajayi and Karyn Watkins's nonprofit organization. They provide year-round education and awareness of the impact of HIV/AIDS on women and girls in their community, as well as on their site.

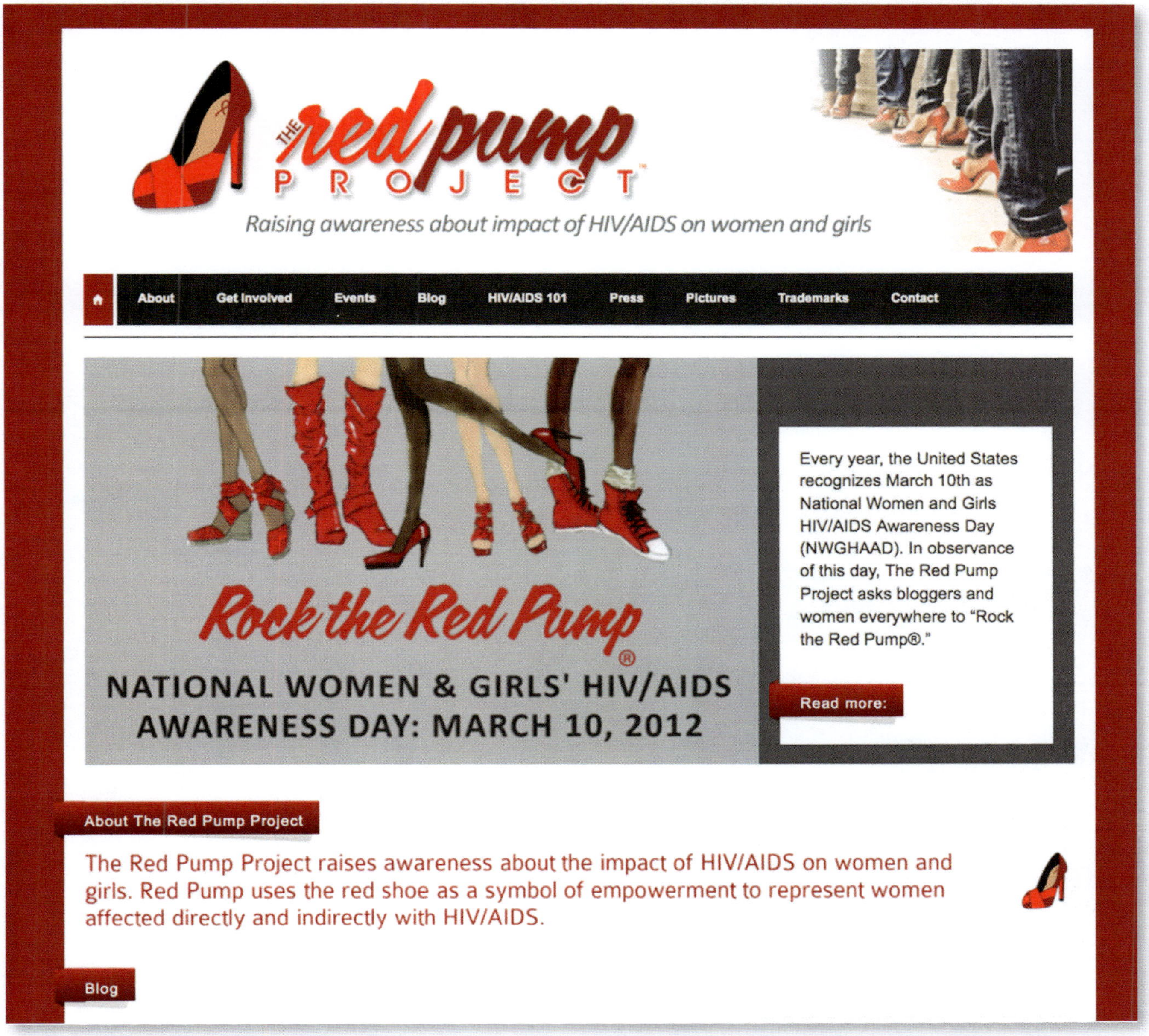

#27 COMMENTS OF READERS

Turn the comments of your readers into blog posts. You'll want to do this for two reasons:

- To show your appreciation for their support
- To show that your site is adding value to the lives of your readers

Pros:

- Highlighting the voices and expertise of your audience will make them feel special
- You don't have to look for content because it's already on your site

Other Considerations:

- Be sure you quote directly and do not change or dilute the actual meaning of the person's statement
- Use comments as testimonials or to start conversations

SAMPLE POST CREATED FROM COMMENTS OF READERS

On my community site, Shorty: Your Chicago South Side Resource, I wrote a post stating that I could not find any information on Fun Town, the last neighborhood amusement park in Chicago. Mr. Lee happened upon my site and kindly shared his memories in the comments section. I made it the subject of a post, and it has become the most popular topic on my site.

#28 GRATITUDE/THANK YOU

Saying "thank you" is not only common courtesy, but it is also a small deed with great impact. Imagine how a person would feel if you wrote an entire post, even if only a few words, expressing your gratitude.

Pros:

- The entire world can see your appreciation for the person
- Make a big impact on someone's day with a small act

Other Considerations:

- Write general and specific "thank you messages" to your readers and supporters every now and then
- Everyone doesn't want their picture online; be sure to get permission before posting
- Ask the person that's being honored to share the link to the story with people on their e-mail lists and social networking sites. This will drive traffic to your site
- Extend your creativity by using multimedia tools

SAMPLE THANK YOU POST

Sharon Hurley Hall thanked fellow writers, bloggers, and other supporters who helped her along her blogging journey on her site, Get Paid to Write Online. This was a great way for her to express her gratitude to a group of people at one time; give exposure to other professionals and their ventures; and highlight the value that they added to her life. Her honorees can share this information as testimonials on their sites.

GETPAIDTOWRITEONLINE
Straight talk about the writing biz

Home | About | Start Here | Freelance Writing Advice | Resources | Write For Us | Contact | Sitemap

You are here: Home › writing › Thankful – Without Thanksgiving

SHARON HURLEY HALL — NOVEMBER 24, 2011

Thankful – Without Thanksgiving

Where I come from, we don't celebrate Thanksgiving. We have the turkey, feasting and holiday trimmings a bit later in the year. Yet, it never hurts to be thankful. I believe in having an attitude of gratitude. As well as being thankful for relatively good health and the ability to make a living doing what I love, I am grateful for a whole bunch of people who have inspired or supported me (sometimes both) since I started blogging.

George Angus is part of the Get Paid to Write Online community. I swear he shares practically everything that's written on this blog and stops by my Facebook page to like it too. Thanks, George.

Fellow writers who have inspired me with their professionalism, skill and willingness to give good, no-nonsense advice include Deb Ng, Anne Wayman, Lori

GET OUR FREE NEWSLETTER

FREE ebook when you subscribe to our FREE newsletter

Business School of Hard Knocks: Real-Life Cautionary Tales

Name:

Email:

Sign up!

We respect your email privacy

Powered by AWeber Email Newsletters

#29 BOAST POSTS

This is your chance to celebrate your successes, as well as those of others.

Pros:

- Everyone loves good news, so share big and small successes
- It's okay to boast about yourself every now and then; your readers will get to know you better

Other Consideration:

- Remember, there is a difference between boasting and bragging. Boasting is humbly sharing your accomplishments and the successes of others with your online family. Bragging is making self-centered announcements that are only about you, all the time. Humility looks good on you.

SAMPLE BOAST POST

Melinda Emerson, better known as SmallBiz Lady, has much to boast about. In this post, she was celebrating three years of helping early entrepreneurs through her weekly Twitter talk show, #SmallBizChat, which is one of Twitter's longest-running chats.

Her other accolades include authoring a bestselling book, *Become Your Own Boss in 12 Months: A Month-by-Month Guide to a Business That Works*, as well as being named the #1 Woman for Entrepreneurs to Follow on Twitter by *Forbes* Magazine.

SmallBizLady
Melinda Emerson

HOME About Blog Products Calendar Services #SmallBizChat Press Contact Us

Smallbizchat Celebrates 3 Years of Helping Thousands of Entrepreneurs

by Melinda Emerson on April 25, 2012 in Business Inspiration, Melinda Emerson @SmallBizLady, SmallBizChat

SmallBiz Chat with Melinda Emerson

Today marks the third anniversary of my Twitter talk show #Smallbizchat.

We launched the weekly #Smallbizchat, in April of 2009, as a peer-to-peer mentoring program to help early stage entrepreneurs get answers to their small business questions. The goal was to provide information to help end small business failure.Â With 82% of small businesses going out of business in five years, we wanted to do something that would really be impactful by giving people information that, in many cases, they had no idea was critical to their business success.

Nearly 150 shows and over 150K followers later, #SmallBizChat has become an institution on Twitter as one of the longest running tweetchats. @SmallBizChatâ€™s third anniversary show is tonight Wednesday April 25, 2012 from 8-9 pm ET, with guest Alexis Maybank, Co-Founder and Chief Strategy Officer of The Gilt Groupe www.gilt.com, one of the top online members-only shopping websites. Maybank is also the co-author of the new book for entrepreneurs â€œ*By Invitation Only: How We Built Gilt and Changed the Way Millions Shop.*

My inspiration to launch the #Smallbizchat community happened after I wrote my bestselling book â€œ*Become Your Own Boss in 12 months; A Month-by-Month Guide to a Business That Works*â€ (now in its third printing). Even before the book came out, I wanted to reduce the learning curve as individuals attempted to start and grow their small

SEARCH

Search...

Become Your Own Boss In 12 Months

Download your FREE chapter of Become Your Own Boss In 12 Months

Free Chapter

Order a Special Signed Edition now for $16 including shipping.

Add To Cart

Categories

Select Category

Subscribe to My Blog Via Email or RSS Feed

Enter your email address:

Subscribe

Delivered by FeedBurner -

TESTIMONIAL

"Amid the flood of gurus promising blogging nirvana, Marcie Hill's precise, well thought out book is a lifesaver for those stumbling at the start or muddling through. Grab hold of her advice, consider her pointers and swim on to a better day with your Internet life."

Stephen Franklin - Journalism trainer and committed blogger

PART 4

ENGAGE YOUR AUDIENCE

In addition to having a platform to share your thoughts, opinions, and expertise, blogs are great for building community through conversations and engagement. Although conversations are the main way to attract and retain your audience, the following list includes seven additional ways you can engage them:

1. **Contests**
2. **Open Questions/Discussions**
3. **Quizzes**
4. **Survey/Polls**
5. **What If/Hypothetical**
6. **Giveaways**
7. **Projects**

#30 CONTESTS

Contests are one of the easiest ways to engage your audience. They can be as simple as submitting photos or as complex as writing essays. Make them fun, entertaining, and simple. People may not participate if there is too much work involved.

Pro:

- You may get more traffic and audience engagement as the contest progresses

Other Considerations:

- Prizes are the main motivators for your audience, so make them good. They don't have to be expensive, just practical
- Keep the contest simple
- The number of people visiting your site may decline after the contest is over

SAMPLE CONTEST ON BLOG

Dequiana Jackson hosts contests on her site, Entrepreneur Resources: Small Business Blog, where small business owners can answer questions or tell their stories to win gift cards, which are ideal prizes.

#31 OPEN QUESTION/DISCUSSION

The best way to start discussions with your readers is by asking questions. Your inquiries can be topics related to your site or niche; they can also be comments from your audience. Either way, subjects can be fun or formal.

Pros:

- This will increase conversations between you and your readers
- You will learn new information

Other Considerations:

- Depending on the question asked, you may not receive responses
- Be sure to moderate the discussion because you will have to intervene if it gets too heated
- Because blogs are global platforms, you will never know who's reading your work and answering your questions

SAMPLE DISCUSSION ON BLOG

Felicity Fields, the editorial manager at Firepole Marketing, wanted to gauge the readers' feelings about their prices. This conversation was valuable for three reasons. First, everyone had a chance to share their stories. Second, it was discovered that many business owners, freelancers, and consultants questions their prices even after they have determined their rates. And third, it makes you think about prices vs. value offered.

#32 QUIZZES

Have you seen the "What's your IQ?"or "Which Cartoon Character Are You?" quizzes online? These questionnaires are quirky and entertaining ways for people to find out more about themselves.

You can create your own quizzes or borrow from one of the following three sites:

- Quiz Box
- My Quiz Creator
- Blog Quiz

Pros:

- Quizzes are fun additions to your site
- Your audience will be drawn in by the quiz titles

Other Considerations:

- Make your topics relatable and engaging. Visitors may not participate if they cannot relate to the topics
- Ask your readers to submit quizzes or topic ideas
- Be careful not to offend your audience by the quiz topics or questions being asked

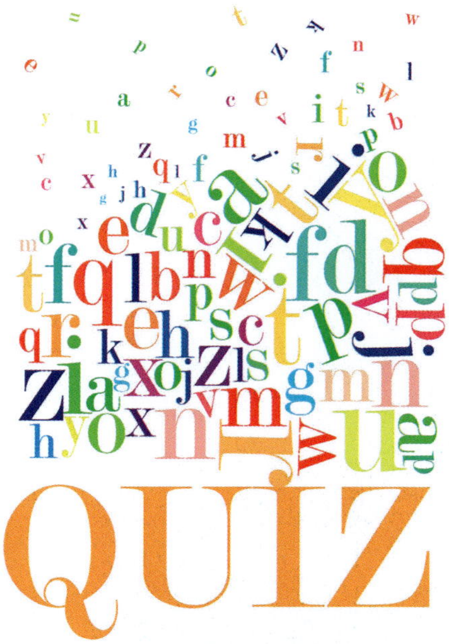

SAMPLE QUIZ SITE

FunQuizCards, an Internet Design Zone property, has several thought-provoking and engaging quizzes to which you can link on your site. It's a quick way to provide content and a fun way to keep readers on your site longer.

#33 SURVEYS/POLLS

Use surveys and polls to get feedback and responses to general or specific questions from your audience. What is the difference between the two? A poll is one question with several possible answers, whereas surveys are more detailed. They may include essay questions, fill-in-the-blank questions, or a combination of both.

You can create polls using sites such as:

- Polldaddy
- Google Docs
- SurveyMonkey

Pro:

- Surveys and polls are great ways to conduct free market research through your audience's responses

Other Considerations:

- Getting people to respond is usually the biggest challenge
- The lack of participation can be discouraging; however, with a little persistence you can get a few responses
- Be sure questions are clearly stated and easily understood
- For formal polls and surveys, provide an explanation of the purpose of the survey and how the responses will be used
- Make the results visible to participants

SAMPLE POLL ON SITE

Sherryl Perry created a survey to find out how her Keep Up with the Web readers were adapting to Google+ after getting mixed reviews about it in a previous post. Note that even though she included the poll in the post, she received more comments on the post than she did survey votes. This is not unusual.

#34 WHAT IF/HYPOTHETICAL

"What if"/Hypotethical posts can range from "nice" subjects to industry topics to absolutely absurd. Even extreme subjects could be thought-provoking.

Following are samples of each type of scenario:

Nice	Would the Blogosphere or Twitterverse be bigger in the offline world?
Industry	Do bloggers earn more than trained journalists?
Absurd	If your pet could speak, what would it say about you?

Pros:

- This is an opportunity to get inside the minds of your audience
- Make serious topics more inviting by presenting them in a light-hearted way

Other Considerations:

- Some comments can be just as off-the-wall as the scenarios, and depending on the response, it could very well become a blog post
- Keep the topics relatable and stay away from controversial subjects like religion, politics, and other divisive issues

SAMPLE "WHAT IF" POST

Philip Bowne of Robotic Rhetoric gave an entertaining, yet thought-provoking insight on "How Long Before Social Media Governs The Planet?" It's very appealing because the online world is invading the offline space.

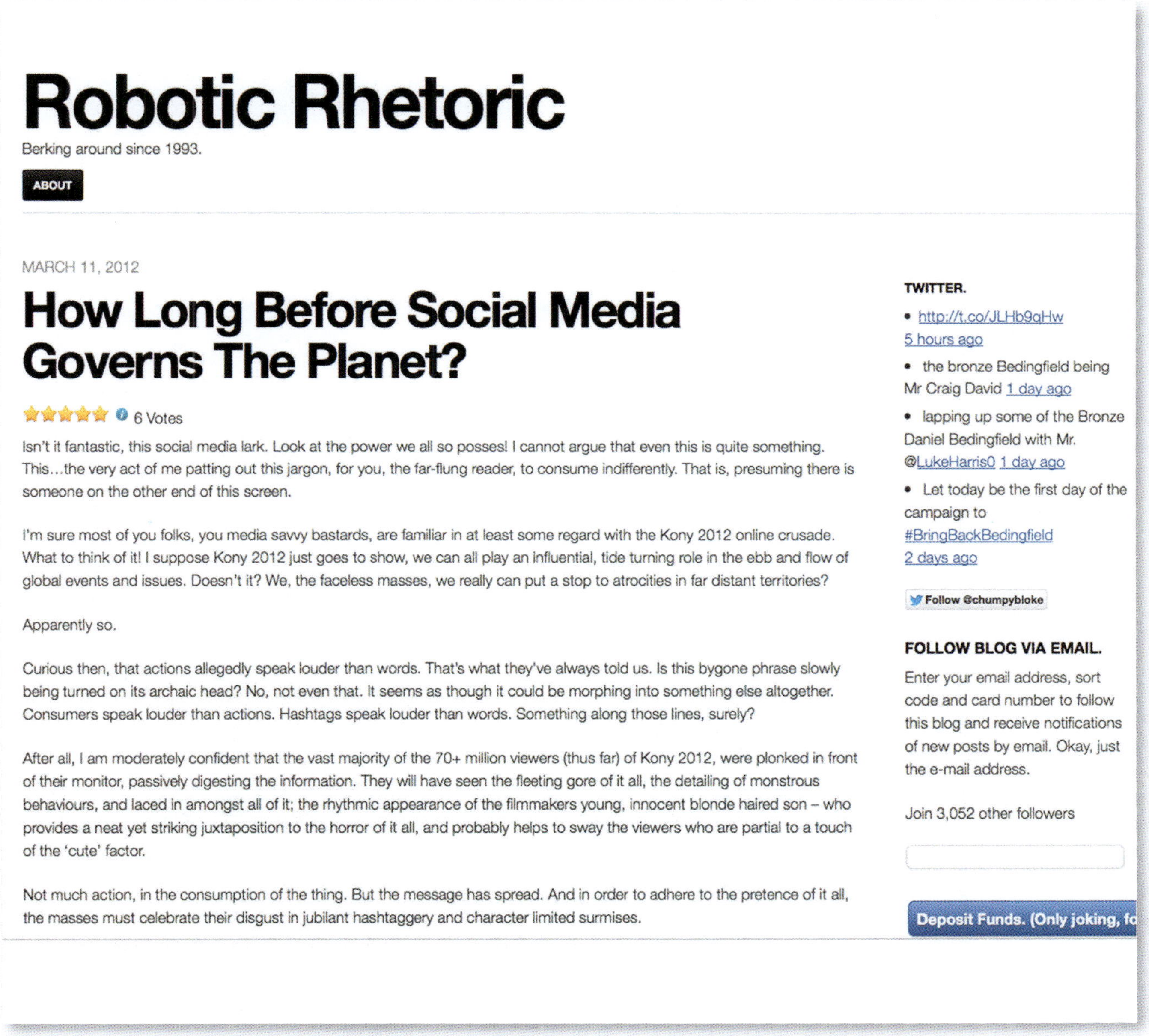

Robotic Rhetoric

Berking around since 1993.

ABOUT

MARCH 11, 2012

How Long Before Social Media Governs The Planet?

6 Votes

Isn't it fantastic, this social media lark. Look at the power we all so posses! I cannot argue that even this is quite something. This…the very act of me patting out this jargon, for you, the far-flung reader, to consume indifferently. That is, presuming there is someone on the other end of this screen.

I'm sure most of you folks, you media savvy bastards, are familiar in at least some regard with the Kony 2012 online crusade. What to think of it! I suppose Kony 2012 just goes to show, we can all play an influential, tide turning role in the ebb and flow of global events and issues. Doesn't it? We, the faceless masses, we really can put a stop to atrocities in far distant territories?

Apparently so.

Curious then, that actions allegedly speak louder than words. That's what they've always told us. Is this bygone phrase slowly being turned on its archaic head? No, not even that. It seems as though it could be morphing into something else altogether. Consumers speak louder than actions. Hashtags speak louder than words. Something along those lines, surely?

After all, I am moderately confident that the vast majority of the 70+ million viewers (thus far) of Kony 2012, were plonked in front of their monitor, passively digesting the information. They will have seen the fleeting gore of it all, the detailing of monstrous behaviours, and laced in amongst all of it; the rhythmic appearance of the filmmakers young, innocent blonde haired son – who provides a neat yet striking juxtaposition to the horror of it all, and probably helps to sway the viewers who are partial to a touch of the 'cute' factor.

Not much action, in the consumption of the thing. But the message has spread. And in order to adhere to the pretence of it all, the masses must celebrate their disgust in jubilant hashtaggery and character limited surmises.

TWITTER.

- http://t.co/JLHb9qHw 5 hours ago
- the bronze Bedingfield being Mr Craig David 1 day ago
- lapping up some of the Bronze Daniel Bedingfield with Mr. @LukeHarris0 1 day ago
- Let today be the first day of the campaign to #BringBackBedingfield 2 days ago

Follow @chumpybloke

FOLLOW BLOG VIA EMAIL.

Enter your email address, sort code and card number to follow this blog and receive notifications of new posts by email. Okay, just the e-mail address.

Join 3,052 other followers

Deposit Funds. (Only joking, fo

#35 GIVEAWAYS

Who doesn't love free stuff? Give something away on your site, but make your readers earn it. Ask them to leave comments on your site; to follow you on Twitter; or to like your Facebook page. Add a sign-up form so you can build your e-mail list. Select a prize that can be used by anyone.

Pros:

- Your traffic and audience engagement will increase
- This is a fun way to engage your readers

Other Considerations:

- Readers may only visit your site because of the giveaway
- Give people more than one option to participate. Everyone is not on Facebook and Twitter and they may not join these sites just to participate in your giveaway
- Provide clear instructions on how to participate
- Award the winner immediately

SAMPLE GIVEAWAY ON SITE

Joel Falcone's Fuel Your Blogging site had a postcard giveaway by one of their sponsors, 1800Postcards.com. This was a win-win for the site and sponsor in three ways:

- Joel had to write about the sponsor's company and their product for his audience, which was exposure for the sponsor.
- The readers had to tell why they should win the cards in the comment section, which boosted the level of engagement on the site.
- The company added the site's visitors to its database by requiring them to enter their contact information to win.

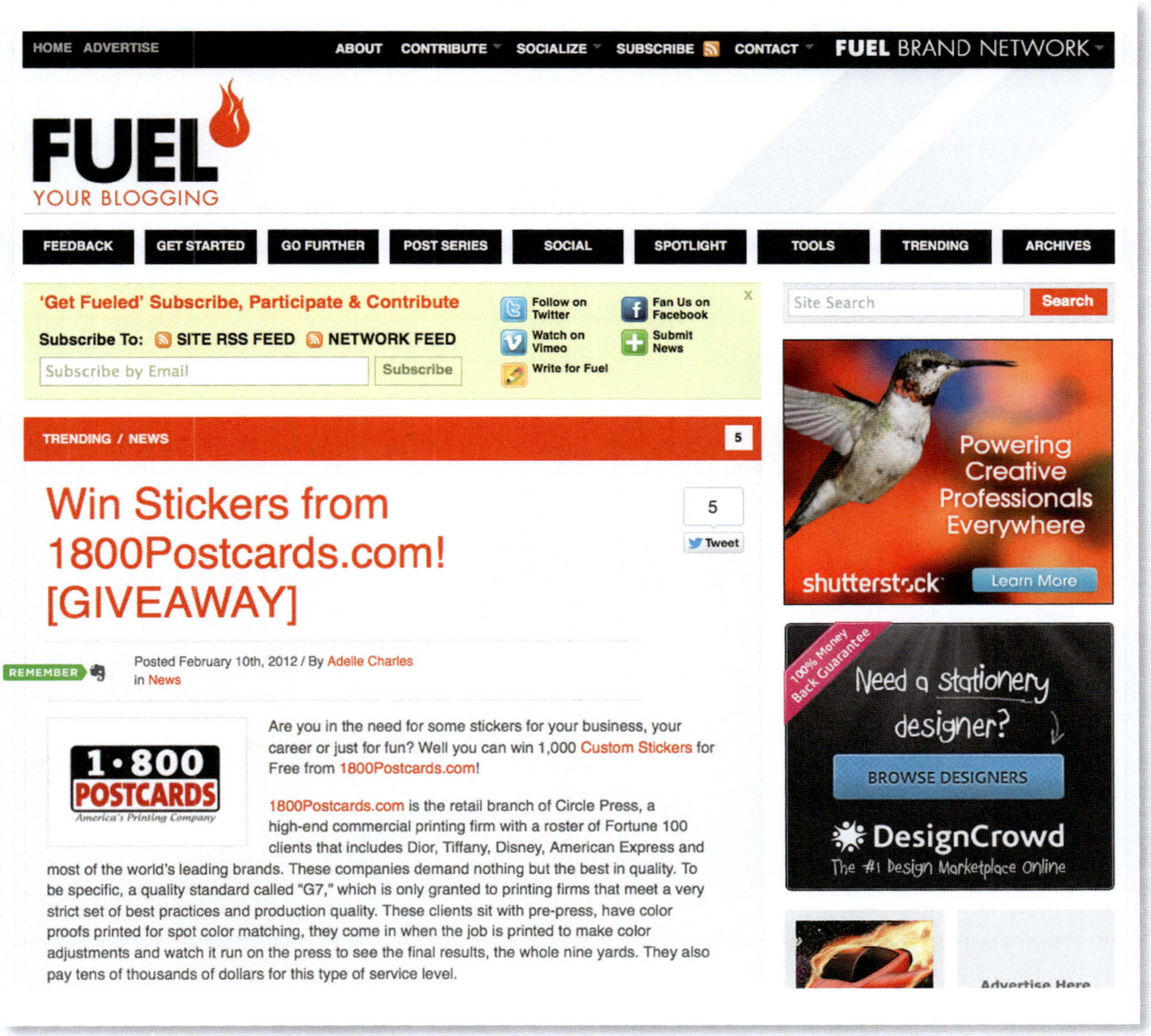

#36 PROJECTS

Let your audience know about projects you are working on or participating in, and invite them to join you. Depending on the type of project, share the results of their efforts on your site. You can also create projects of your own and give your readers assignments.

Pros:

- Having company and support in your endeavors is always a great thing
- Your audience engagement will increase, even if they only serve as virtual cheerleaders

Other Considerations:

- You will probably have more encouragers than participants
- The project must be valuable to your audience in order for them to participate
- As the excitement of the project wanes, so will participation
- When assigning projects, make sure the tasks add value to what your readers are already doing

SAMPLE PROJECT POST

A few years ago, I participated in Blog2Print's Blogapalooza to kick off their new venture. It was a 24-hour blogathon in which participants had to post every hour on their own sites and then add the link to Blog2Print's site. I invited my readers to join me and only one person obliged.

I am pleased to announce that because of this experience, my eBook, *The ABCs of Blogging: Blogging Basics from A to Z*, was written within 24 hours.

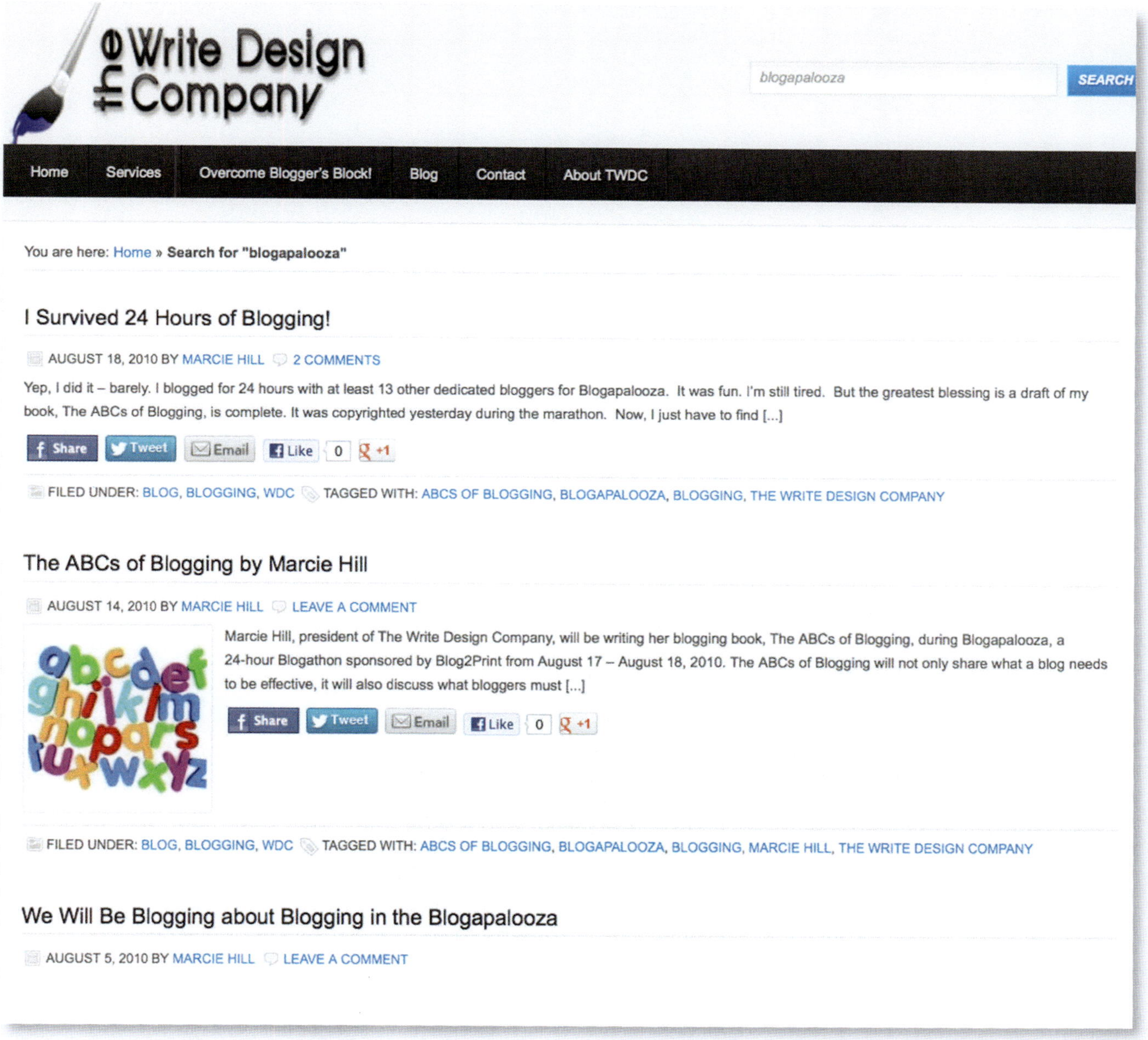

the Write Design Company

blogapalooza SEARCH

Home | Services | Overcome Blogger's Block! | Blog | Contact | About TWDC

You are here: Home » **Search for "blogapalooza"**

I Survived 24 Hours of Blogging!

AUGUST 18, 2010 BY MARCIE HILL 2 COMMENTS

Yep, I did it – barely. I blogged for 24 hours with at least 13 other dedicated bloggers for Blogapalooza. It was fun. I'm still tired. But the greatest blessing is a draft of my book, The ABCs of Blogging, is complete. It was copyrighted yesterday during the marathon. Now, I just have to find [...]

Share Tweet Email Like 0 +1

FILED UNDER: BLOG, BLOGGING, WDC TAGGED WITH: ABCS OF BLOGGING, BLOGAPALOOZA, BLOGGING, THE WRITE DESIGN COMPANY

The ABCs of Blogging by Marcie Hill

AUGUST 14, 2010 BY MARCIE HILL LEAVE A COMMENT

Marcie Hill, president of The Write Design Company, will be writing her blogging book, The ABCs of Blogging, during Blogapalooza, a 24-hour Blogathon sponsored by Blog2Print from August 17 – August 18, 2010. The ABCs of Blogging will not only share what a blog needs to be effective, it will also discuss what bloggers must [...]

Share Tweet Email Like 0 +1

FILED UNDER: BLOG, BLOGGING, WDC TAGGED WITH: ABCS OF BLOGGING, BLOGAPALOOZA, BLOGGING, MARCIE HILL, THE WRITE DESIGN COMPANY

We Will Be Blogging about Blogging in the Blogapalooza

AUGUST 5, 2010 BY MARCIE HILL LEAVE A COMMENT

TESTIMONIALS

"We ALL bump into 'blogger's block' -- even those of us who've been writing professionally for decades. In this book, Marcie Hill not only gives us ideas for getting unstuck and creating highly readable posts, but she offers great Posts on building true ENGAGEMENT with our readers -- something every blogger must do to stay relevant."

Maureen Jenkins, Travel & Food Writer/Consultant

PART 5

YOU'RE THE AUTHORITY

Your blog is a great way to establish yourself as an authority on your topic. Sometimes you set out to do this intentionally, other times it happens by accident. Either way, it doesn't happen overnight. Following are five ways your site can position you as an expert:

1. **Advice**
2. **Reviews**
3. **FAQs**
4. **Problem/Solution**
5. **Comparison**

#37 ADVICE

There are at least three ways to establish your authority through advice:

- Create a site completely dedicated to giving advice on a specific topic
- Give advice on your site's topics one day a week
- Write informational, how-to, and quick posts about subjects on your site or in your industry

Pros:

- Your credibility as an authority will increase
- Expand your knowledge by researching and reporting different topics

Other Consideration:

- Provide advice on one or two topics initially, become known as an expert at those, and then venture into other subjects
- You can control how people perceive you

SAMPLE ADVICE SITE

Amy Clark's blog, Mom Advice, provides resources and advice on topics important to mommies - from saving money, to products, to food.

Love and relationships have always been hot topics, but they are even hotter these days with extremely high divorce rates and individuals living the single life. Husband and wife team, Susie & Otto Collins, created a business around providing advice on love and relationships.

Love and Relationship Advice Blog

Susie and Otto Collins, Relationship Coaches, Authors, and Speakers

OCTOBER 01, 2012

» Enter our Facebook contest and win one of our relationship programs!

We're GIVING AWAY one of our programs to 3 lucky people who answer a very simple question.

Between now and Wednesday 10/312, post on our Susie and Otto Collins Facebook wall your answer to this question:

"What's something your partner has said or done (with clothes on) that made you feel more intimate, close and connected?"

On Wed. 10/3/12 at midnight, we'll choose the top 3 responses and winners will receive their choice of 1 of our relationship products. You can let your friends know about this contest too!

If you haven't "liked" our Facebook page, click here to "like" the page and answer our question.

If you have "liked" our page before, you'll go directly to the page where you can answer our question.

We're excited to hear what keeps your relationship juicy and alive--and we're excited to possibly share one of our programs with you!

Posted by Susie and Otto Collins at 02:31 PM | Permalink | Comments (0)

SEPTEMBER 24, 2012

» Wish your partner would love you like he or she used to?

Susie & Otto Collins

Subscribe to our blog's feed

[What is this?]

free e-book

"Passionate Spark Lasting Love"

Plus our Love and Relationships newsletter

Sign up below...

First Name *

Email *

COMPANION GUIDE

A companion guide is available to help you generate ideas for your blog or other creative projects.

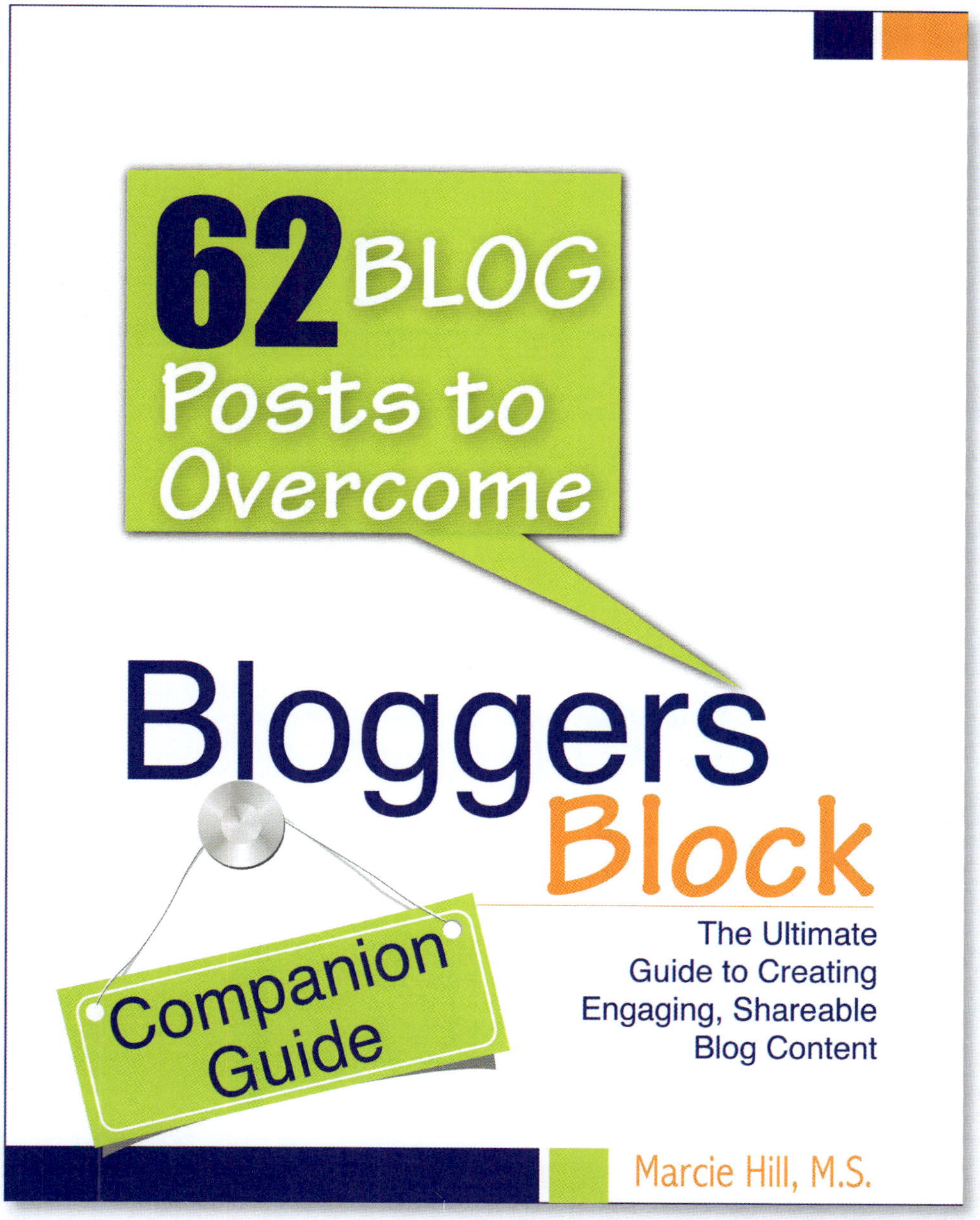

#38 REVIEWS

You can share opinions about people, products, and services for free or for a fee. Be sure to highlight positive and negative factors when writing reviews. Some bloggers are hired by sponsors to write about their products and services, while other bloggers get paid through affiliate programs. Then there are the bloggers that share information just for the love of it.

Pros:

- You can help your audience make buying decisions
- Introduce your readers to products and services that could help make their lives easier and happier

Other Considerations:

- Make helping others, and not getting paid, a priority. It's easy to get caught up in the latter, but if you have to choose, pick people over pay
- Be as honest and objective as possible
- If you are being paid to write reviews, let your audience know. This will not only keep you in compliance with the Federal Trade Commission's disclosure requirements, but it will also let your audience determine the value of your review

SAMPLE REVIEW POST

Hesham Zebida shared a comprehensive review about the Thesis Theme on his site, Famous Bloggers. He objectively shared his opinion about the product and explained why he rated it as he did.

#39 FAQS – FREQUENTLY ASKED QUESTIONS

I'm sure people ask you questions all the time about some aspect of your life: school, work, hobbies, or other interests. Following are three ways to respond to frequently asked questions.

1. Publish individual FAQ posts or list posts from the questions people ask
2. Audio or video record your responses
3. Create screencasts and presentations to craft your responses

Pros:

- You'll never be without content if you turn questions into individual posts
- This is an excellent opportunity to share your expertise

Other Considerations:

- Do not over-share your information. Give just enough "what" so you can get paid for the "how"
- If there is a question you think your audience should have asked, post that, too
- Your FAQ session could become a regular segment on your site
- Consider creating an audio or video segment just for FAQs

SAMPLE FAQ POST

Justin Germino provided a comprehensive post on why Livefyre was going to be the comment system on his site, DragonBlogger. He included a FAQ section, which made it easy for his audience to understand how the new system worked and the impact it had on previous comments.

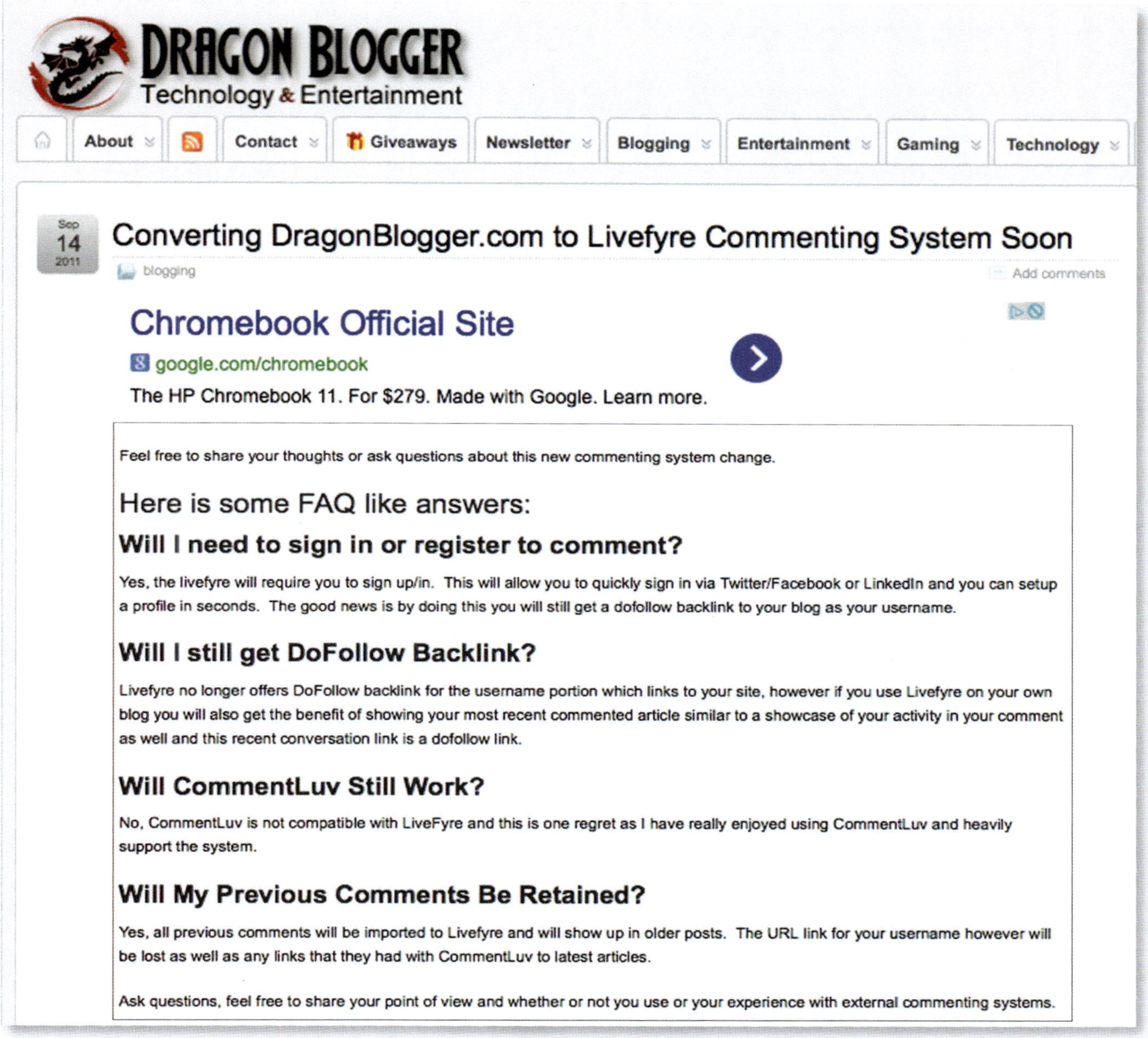

#40 PROBLEM/SOLUTION

You will always encounter problems and challenges in some aspect of your life. It is perfectly okay to share them on your site. In fact, you can engage your readers by asking them what they would do in the face of that challenge. Or, use the challenge as a teachable moment by providing solutions and lessons learned.

For the ultimate engagement, encourage your readers to submit or post problems they are experiencing and ask the audience members for solutions.

Pros:

- You can bring issues to the forefront and give your readers solutions on how to correct them
- You will give your readers something to think about
- You are providing a platform for your audience to share their problems

Other Considerations:

- By not providing solutions, you may come across as a whiner
- Do not over-share personal information
- Spotlighting your problem may help someone that is going through a similar predicament
- Encouraging your audience to share their problems may help them unload a burden

SAMPLE PROBLEM/SOLUTION POST

Readers of Blogging Pro, a Splashpress Media creation, are drawn in to posts because they always begin with a story to which they can relate. They are then presented with blogging pitfalls related to the story, as well as tips and resources on how to avoid them. This is one of the unique elements of the posts on this site.

#41 COMPARISON

A comparison is a review of two or more similar things. These posts are most effective when you:

1. Provide a background on the items being compared
2. Explain the factors you are comparing and why
3. Highlight the good and bad features of each of them

Pros:

- You will come across as an authority depending on how you present the information
- This can become profitable for you

Other Considerations:

- Do not give people too many options when comparing. Try to keep the number small, yet practical
- Try to compare "like" things. For instance, it would be a disservice to your audience to compare a camcorder and digital camera; however, it wouldn't be too farfetched to compare a camcorder and webcam
- Use tables and other visuals so that readers can see the difference between the items being compared

SAMPLE COMPARISON POST

In this post on ProBlogging Success, Jane Sheeba compares blogging to tweeting and provides arguments on why the former is better.

ProBlogging Success

Cutting-edge, no BS strategies to achieve blogging success, the professional way - with Jane Sheeba

About Blog Products Services FREE E-Books Resources

Get started with your journey as a Problogger

- Actionable (no fluff) tips to make your blog successful!
- Cutting-edge strategies (not just tactics)!
- Solution to your blogging problems, right away!

Exclusive blogging tips directly to your inbox!

Email:

Get Free Instant Access

Do You Know Why Tweeting Cannot Replace Blogging?

by JANE SHEEBA / Join Jane on Google+

Blogging is a new form of media today. No one knows exactly when people started to blog, but since then the blogosphere (the world of blogs and bloggers) has evolved so much. There has been thousands of thousand blog since then and there are hundreds of blogs started every day. People choose to blog for so many reasons which include fun, personal log, sharing with friends, make money (and this will include all sorts of advertising revenues, product launches, selling own products, affiliate business and so on), establish online presence, share knowledge and so on.

Twitter is another online evolution or revolution which has attracted millions of people. People who sell, who buy, who look for information and who share information assemble there and tweet, tweet and tweet. Bloggers especially use Twitter to let their followers know about their blogs, or in other words, they use *Twitter as their tool of promotion.*

There are lots of people who debate on the pros and cons of both blogging and tweeting. There has been lots of comparative discussion on this topic in the direction of which one is better. From my own perspective, I give below 3 reasons why tweeting cannot replace blogging.

The 140 limitation:

Yes, as everyone knows, Twitter implements the 140 character policy. You can only post a tweet not exceeding 140 characters; this also applies to direct

What's Hot Now?

25 Quick Social Media Tricks And Ideas For Bloggers

Email List Building: A 3 Step Working Strategy To Build Email List FAST

How To Be An Un-Annoying Blogger (You Don't Have To Please Everyone)

How To Beat The "Not Writing" Block And Publish Awesome Content

To search, type and hit enter

Never Miss a Blog Post!

Enter your email address:

Subscribe

Subscribe for blog updates (not the newsletter).

DON'T MISS OUT, SIGN UP TODAY

Would you like tips on how to create content that will get more shares on Facebook, Twitter, LinkedIn, Google+, YouTube, and your other social sites?

Go to www.overcomingbloggersblock.com to sign up for updates.

PART 6

YOU'RE THE RESOURCE

One of the primary functions of a blog is to educate your audience. Blogging can position you as a resource, which helps build your expert status and credibility. There are three types of posts that can help establish you as a resource:

1. **Events**
2. **Opportunities**
3. **Special Reports**

#42 EVENTS

Your site could be THE place to check when events are being held-from parties, to fundraisers, to conferences. You could be THE person to let people know what's going on during events via live blogging, live tweeting, or live streaming. Also, you can give a final report on what happened afterwards.

Use your site to promote events; create a calendar where people can post their own stuff; or highlight the people who will be attending. You can do this for free or for a fee. You can also interview guests at these events for additional insights and comments.

Pros:

- Posting about events will give you more content for your site
- You may become an "accidental" socialite or local celebrity. At the very least, you will become the "go to" person for events

Other Considerations:

- You may experience invitation overload
- People will start inviting you to events because they want you to cover their events, not because they want you to attend for social and leisure purposes
- When your site becomes popular, you may have to charge to provide event coverage via live blogging, live tweeting, and live streaming
- Interviewing celebrities prior to the event will help promote them, your site, and the event
- Small events need love, too. Giving attention to small and new events and venues could result in great payoffs

SAMPLE SITE WITH EVENTS

Country Music Chicago is an excellent resource site. Scott Winterroth, the creator of the site, has done a great job at positioning his site as THE go-to spot for virtually everything related to country music in the big city.

#43 OPPORTUNITIES

Scholarships, jobs, and workshops are just a few of the opportunities that you can share with your audience. Use your platform to help elevate others in their personal and professional lives.

Pros:

- You will be blessed by blessing others
- People will send information to you; you won't have to search for it

Other Considerations:

- Due to time constraints and other commitments, you probably won't be able to share everything people send
- Even though you are merely the messenger, people will ask you details about the information you're sharing; direct them to your site. This is a great way to build traffic

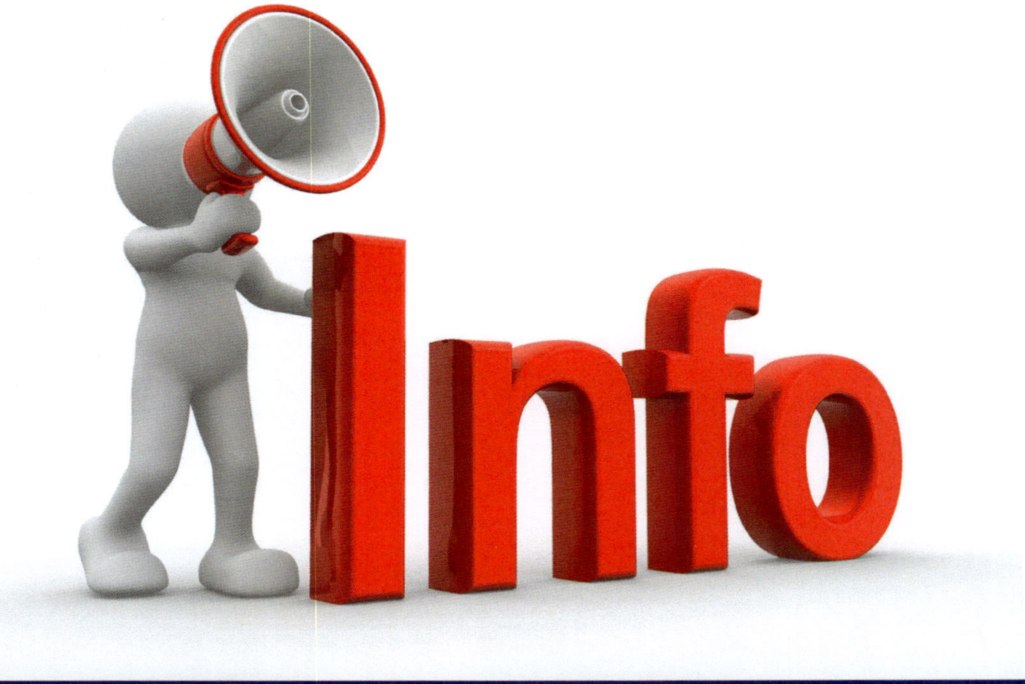

SAMPLE OPPORTUNITIES POST

Freelance writing guru, Anne Wayman, shares her expertise and resources on her site, About Freelance Writing. One of her most valuable offerings is the jobs list for freelance writers. She not only links to the sites, but she also provides feedback.

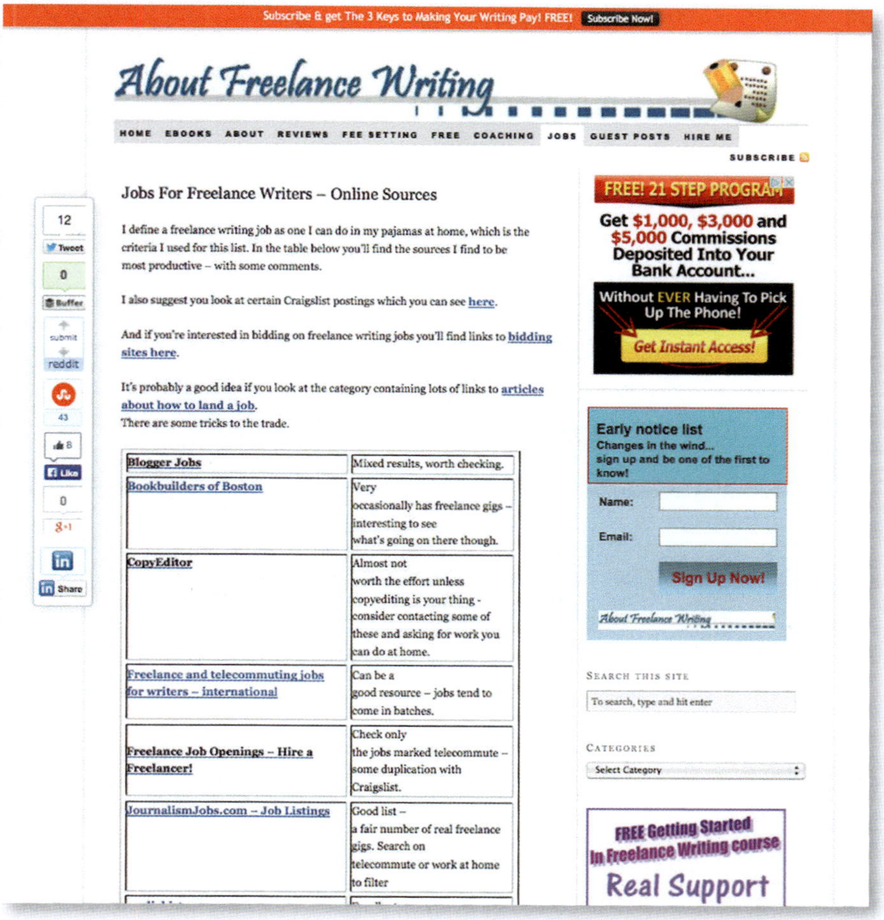

#44 SPECIAL REPORTS

Special reports are information documents, usually shared free of charge, that focus on a singular topic. They come in a variety of "flavors", including, but not limited to:

1. A single page document
2. A multi-page report
3. A small eBook

Sometimes the headline will read "Special Report"; many times it won't.

Pros:

- Special reports tend to drive traffic to your site
- They contribute to the building of your expert status
- The report could be the beginning of a book, program, or a host of other income-generating products
- This is a good way to build your e-mail list

Other Considerations:

- Make sure the report is relevant and valuable to your audience
- The length of reports will vary. If you can educate your audience in five pages, do it. It is a disservice to you and your readers to stretch a simple topic to 20 pages

SAMPLE SPECIAL REPORT

Amazing Women in History is not a special report, per se. But having detailed information delivered directly to readers' e-mailboxes about women who have made valuable contributions to society and have not been recognized, makes it a special report. It is obvious that KeriLynn Engel, the site's owner, is committed to researching and sharing this information.

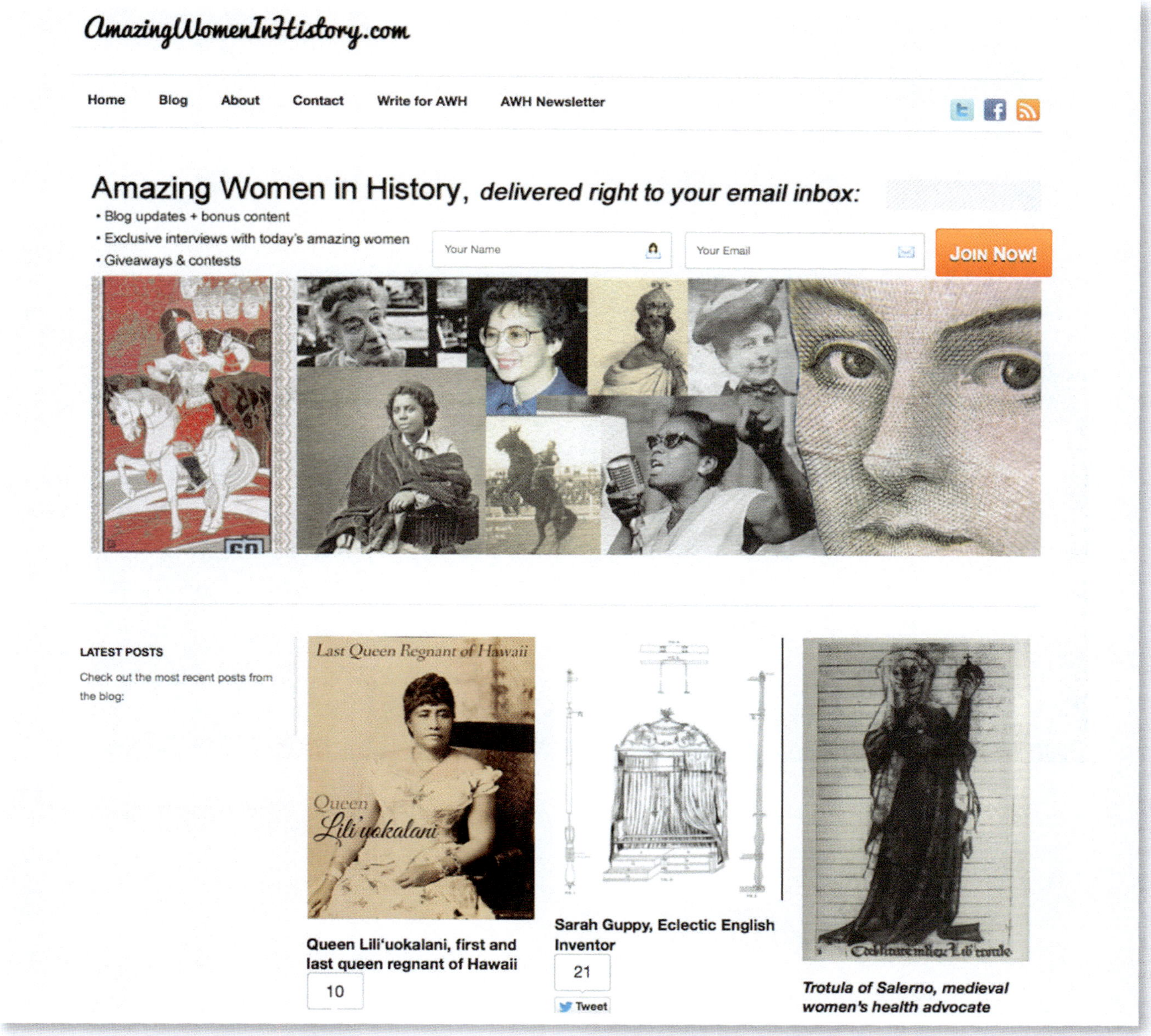

DON'T MISS OUT, SIGN UP TODAY

Get tips, tools, and strategies from other bloggers on how to produce shareable content.

Go to www.overcomingbloggersblock.com to sign up for updates.

PART 7

HUMOR

Who doesn't like to laugh? Humor is always a great way to lighten up any site or situation, as well as brighten someone's mood. You may not always get a big belly laugh, but smiles and chuckles are good for the heart. Topics do not have to be directly related to the subjects on your site. Also, adding humor to your site shows the lighter side of your personality.

Add a little funny to your site with these four types of humorous posts:

1. **Just Plain Ol' Funny**
2. **Parody**
3. **Comics**
4. **Jokes**

#45 JUST PLAIN OL' FUNNY

Some people are naturally funny or extremely witty. On the other hand, there are people who need a little help to kick start their funny bone, but once they get started, they are on a roll. How could anyone NOT appreciate a great sense of humor?

Pros:

- It's always a good feeling to make someone smile, laugh, or chuckle
- Humor tends to be a reflection of a pleasant personality, which attracts more people

Other Considerations:

- Everyone doesn't have a natural sense of humor. If this applies to you, stick to the other 60+ types of blog posts in this book
- Make sure everyone can relate to your topics

SAMPLE PLAIN OL' FUNNY SITE

The Regected Riter is one of the funniest sites online. A.G., the creator of the site, has a wonderful sense of humor and uses his drawings and other multimedia tools to enhance his messages. Although his site was created to relay his tales of rejection as a writer, anyone who has ever been rejected can relate.

Note: This site has not be updated recently due to A.G.'s busy work schedule, but it is still worth visiting.

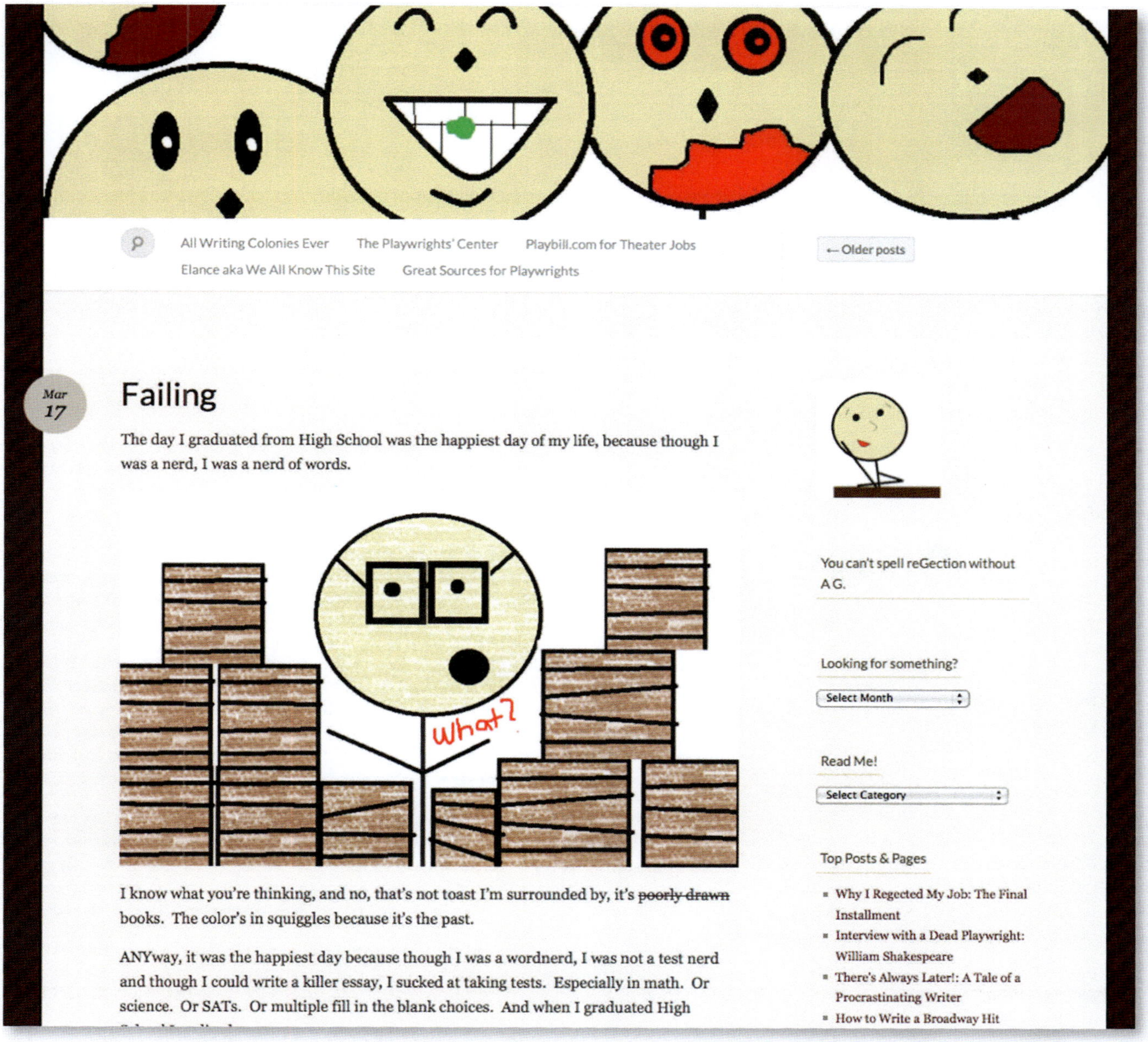

#46 PARODY

Parody, also called satire or spoofs, is the art of making fun of or mocking something, usually with sarcasm or irony. Although they are usually found on political and celebrity sites, they can be a pleasant addition to your site if done well. If creating parody is not your thing, you can always borrow videos and cartoons, or link to other sites.

Pros:

- Your audience will be entertained
- You can build relationships with other content creators by sharing their creations on your site. Be sure to get permission to do so

Other Considerations:

- You may be challenged with creating these posts if you've never done them before
- Your post could result in negative comments if your topic is taken to an extreme or if it is perceived in a certain way
- Depending on the content of the post, disclaimers may be needed
- Be sure to give credit when borrowing other people's work

SAMPLE PARODY SITE

The ONION is one of the best parody publications ever. In addition to being satirical, the writers add humorous twists to factual information. You are guaranteed to find thought-provoking and engaging topics that will make you laugh.

A.V. CLUB | Store | Dating | YouTube: Sex House | Parameter Contest

67° Afternoon: Delight
Onion Weather Center

the ONION®
America's Finest News Source

Search

HOME | VIDEO | POLITICS | SPORTS | ENTERTAINMENT | NEWS BEAT | ECONOMY | SCI/TECH | LOCAL

LATEST NEWS ▶ Armstrong's Space Crap | 32-Minute Nonstop Work Streak | Loose First-Grader | iPhone 5 | Waddling, Chubby Family | Baby Nathan

Study Finds Newborn Infants Can Tell If Parents Are Losers

MARCH 21, 2012 | ISSUE 48•12 | MORE NEWS IN BRIEF

CHICAGO—A study published this week in the journal *Pediatrics* found that, within seconds of their birth, babies have the ability to sense whether their parents are losers. "From the moment they open their eyes, newborns can tell if their mother had no other options and was forced to settle for their father, or if their father is a sad sack who has no friends and gets drunk on a single glass of chardonnay," said researcher Dr. Stuart Lindstrom, explaining that despite their blurry vision, infants can still identify basic loser body types, and have specialized olfactory receptors allowing them to detect the odor of failure. "In fact, we've determined that as early as the second trimester, a fetus picks up on the income and social standing of its mother via the umbilical cord." The study also concluded that the screams of newborns stem from the sudden realization they will be stuck with their loser parents for at least 18 years.

ARTICLE TOOLS
Tweet 756
Like 11k
+1 337
tumblr +

RELATED ARTICLES
Bumbling Astronauts Caught in Wacky 'Lunch-Launch' Mix-up

RECENT VIDEOS
Joe Biden Hitchhikes To Democratic National Convention
Nauseatingly Precious NYC Couples To Walk Around In Rain
Teacher Hoping Students Can Tell He Was Once Popular

ALL NEW SEASON
IT'S ALWAYS SUNNY IN PHILADELPHIA
OCT 11 THURS 10 FX
#SunnyFX

FEATURED SECTION: POLITICS
PARAMETER A.V. SHORT FILM COMPETITION

DAILY NEWSFEED
Eating Rest Of Thing Way Easier Than Putting It Away

SAMPLE PARODY SITE

Written by anonymous police officers, you can get current information about things happening with Chicago's Finest in a sarcastic, and sometimes witty, manner. Ironically, you can get more details about what's happening in Chi-Town from this site than from larger news sources.

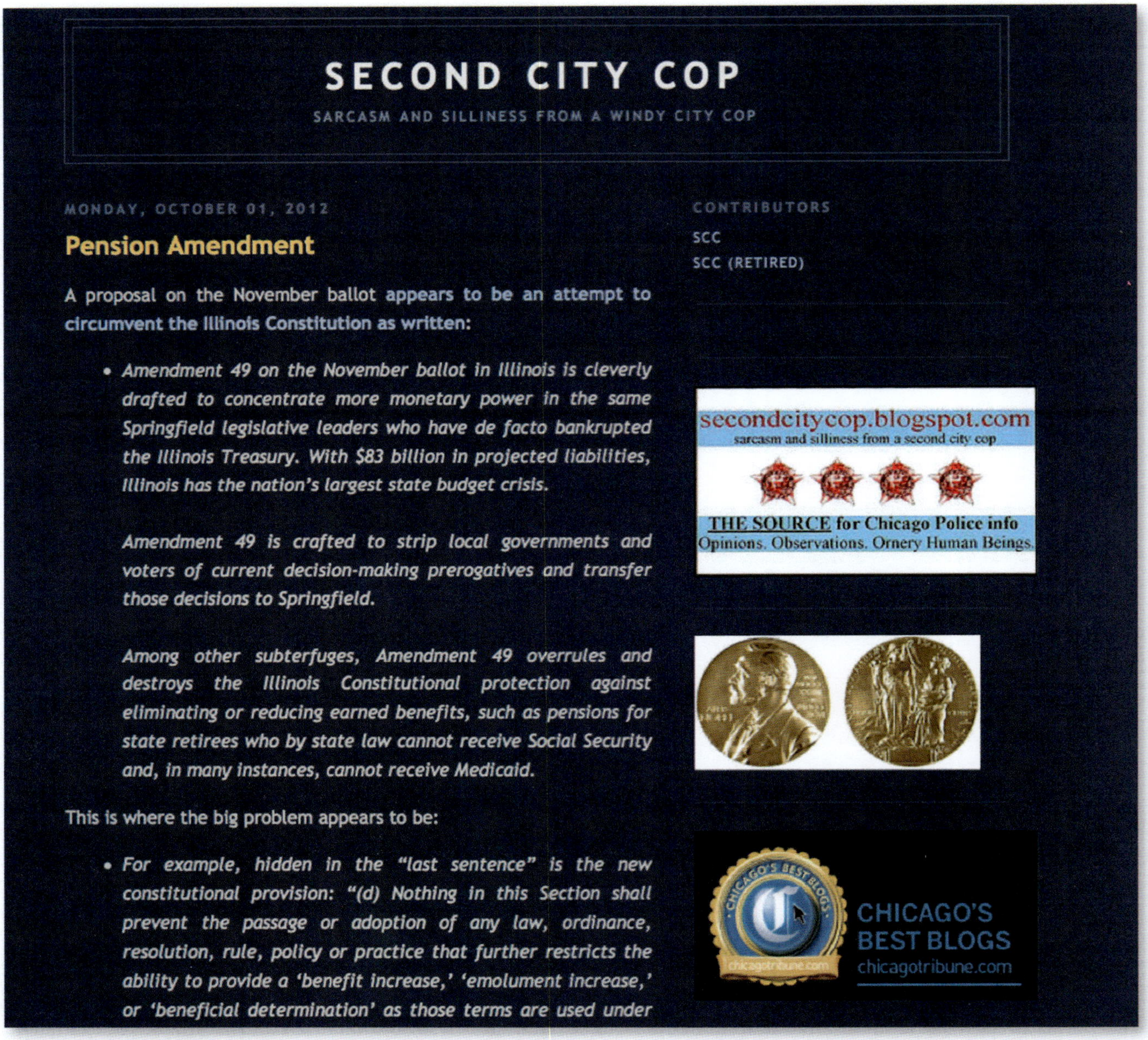

SECOND CITY COP

SARCASM AND SILLINESS FROM A WINDY CITY COP

MONDAY, OCTOBER 01, 2012

Pension Amendment

A proposal on the November ballot appears to be an attempt to circumvent the Illinois Constitution as written:

- *Amendment 49 on the November ballot in Illinois is cleverly drafted to concentrate more monetary power in the same Springfield legislative leaders who have de facto bankrupted the Illinois Treasury. With $83 billion in projected liabilities, Illinois has the nation's largest state budget crisis.*

  Amendment 49 is crafted to strip local governments and voters of current decision-making prerogatives and transfer those decisions to Springfield.

  Among other subterfuges, Amendment 49 overrules and destroys the Illinois Constitutional protection against eliminating or reducing earned benefits, such as pensions for state retirees who by state law cannot receive Social Security and, in many instances, cannot receive Medicaid.

This is where the big problem appears to be:

- *For example, hidden in the "last sentence" is the new constitutional provision: "(d) Nothing in this Section shall prevent the passage or adoption of any law, ordinance, resolution, rule, policy or practice that further restricts the ability to provide a 'benefit increase,' 'emolument increase,' or 'beneficial determination' as those terms are used under*

CONTRIBUTORS

SCC

SCC (RETIRED)

DON'T MISS OUT, SIGN UP TODAY

Be first to know about new books, trainings, and products.

Go to www.overcomingbloggersblock.com to sign up for updates.

#47 COMICS

Comics are a sequence of drawings used to tell a story. You can stretch your level of creativity by making your own or borrowing from someone else. There are two resources that can help you get started:

- Pixton
- Toondoo

Pros:

- Comics can be fun, engaging, and thought-provoking
- They add another level of creativity and skill to your repertoire

Other Considerations:

- Humor is completely subjective. Not everyone will think everything is funny
- Get permission or give credit when borrowing other people's work
- Keep the comic simple and topics relatable
- They may be time consuming to create

SAMPLE COMICS SITE

On Crunchy Crunchy Biscuits, Phil Barry shares random thoughts through comics. He admits that it's his way "of telling sometimes funny jokes" and that "it's not for everyone." His courage to share his thoughts and works with the public is admirable. Are you up for the challenge?

#48 JOKES

Everyone enjoys a good joke. They can be as simple as a one-liner or as long as a full story. Whichever you choose, be sure the topic is one that everyone can relate to and keep it simple. You can try your hand at writing jokes or borrow someone else's.

Pros:

- Jokes help lighten the mood of any site or post
- You can expand your creative imagination

Other Considerations:

- Telling jokes may not be your strength, but try it at least once
- Respect copyright laws when borrowing other people's work

SAMPLE JOKE SITE

Get a daily dose of jokes from Smilezilla. Created by Vladimir Nesterenko and his team, readers can submit jokes and funny stories that can be rated by their peers.

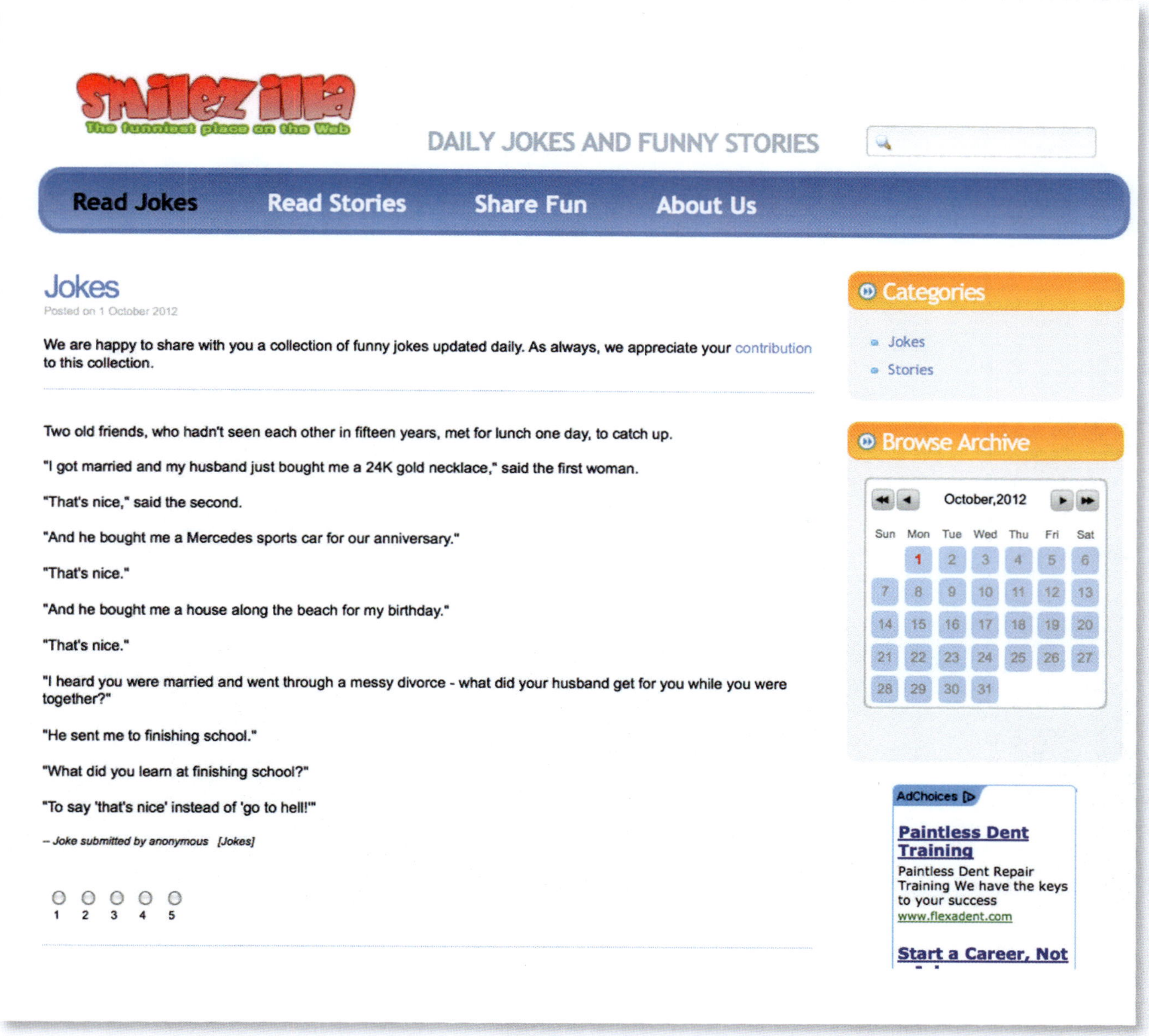

DON'T MISS OUT, SIGN UP TODAY

To link to the actual posts in each of the categories
go to www.overcomingbloggersblock.com to sign up for updates.

PART 8

NEWS AND VIEWS

News articles are typically found on news sites. Many of these sites are either:

- Extensions of print publications,
- Started by laid-off journalists, or
- Community news sources

Also, they tend to fall under three categories:

1. **Hyperlocal**
2. **Long-Form Journalism**
3. **Editorials**

Did you know that these posts can be found on blog sites?

#49 HYPERLOCAL

Many hyperlocal sites provide news and stories about the community, relevant to the people in the community, written by people who live in the community.

These sites are sometimes created from someone's desire to share local news. Often they result from the lack of, or incorrect, coverage by mainstream media and newspapers.

You can build a site around a geographical area and topics relevant to those areas; you don't have to share news. Or, you can focus on one or more facets of the community: arts, culture, events, family activities, employment, or education.

Pros:

- When information about a community is written by people that are a part of that community, they are able to relate to the needs of the readers and share information that is relevant to them
- More people in the community can get their voices heard by contributing to the site
- Your site may become THE source of community news

Other Considerations:

- You have to be ready to reject or tutor people who want to contribute but lack writing skills
- Try to diversify your content by using text, images, audio, and video
- Because most hyperlocal sites are run by volunteers, it may be challenging to get reliable assistance
- You may get backlash for being the bearer of bad news or for not sharing news at all
- If you grow to become THE voice of the community, people may look to you to represent the entire community

SAMPLE HYPERLOCAL SITE

The Welles Park Bulldog is a model hyperlocal site that shares news and stories about the Lincoln Square, Ravenswood, and North Center communities in Chicago. Created by Patrick Boylan, a trained journalist who cares about the community, it is professionally written, easy to read and navigate. This site can easily compete with larger online news publications.

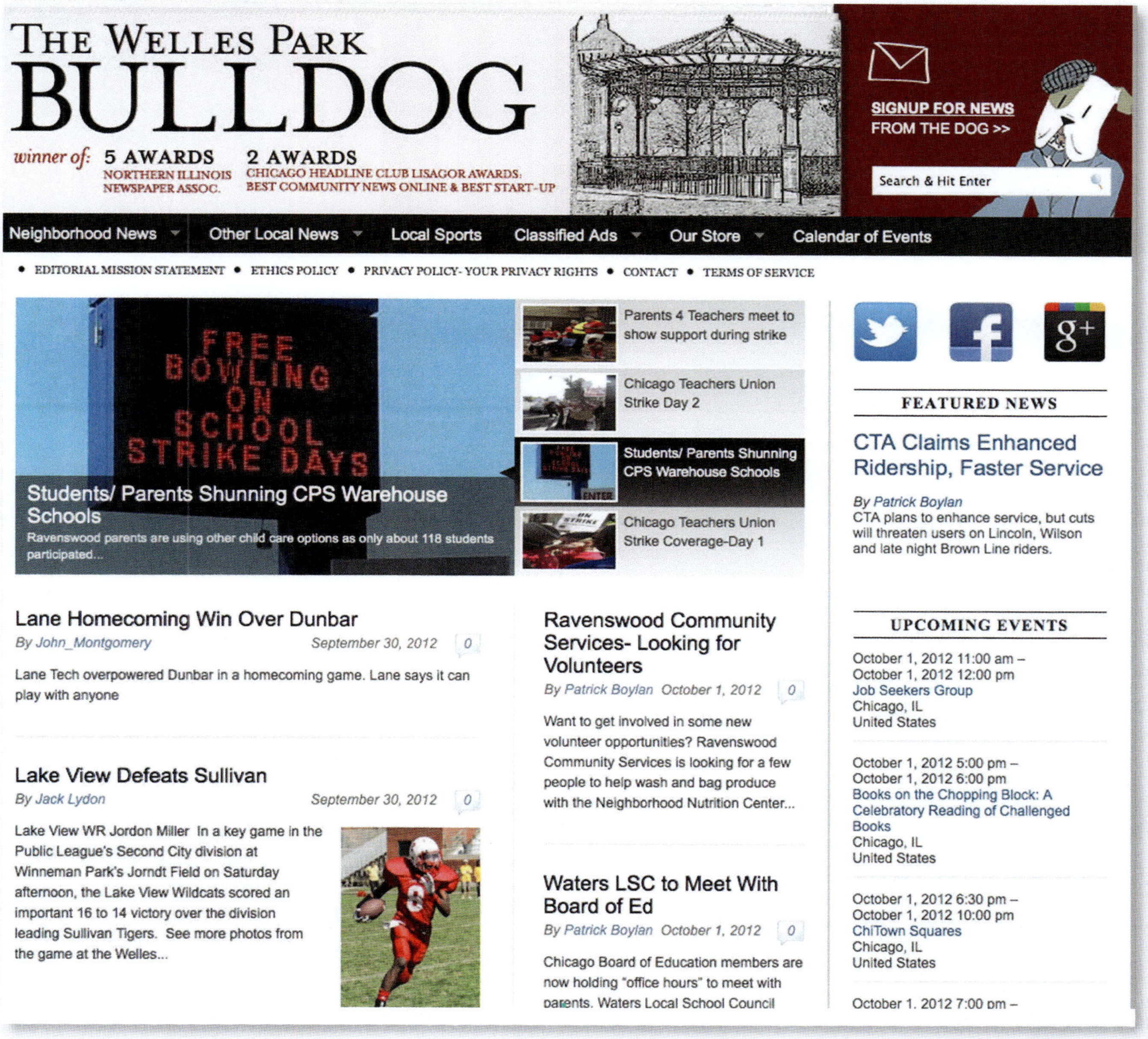

SAMPLE HYPERLOCAL SITE

My community site, Shorty: Your Chicago South Side Resource, is a hyperlocal site that spotlights the people, communities, history, and events on the he South Side of Chicago. It was also created to counter the negative images and tales that are common on local news stations.

HOME ABOUT SHORTY HIRE SHORTY CONTACT

Search this website... GO!

Go Shorty

Your Chicago South Side Resource for Culture, Education, Employment, Health and Young People

CLASSICS CULTURE EDUCATION EMPLOYMENT HEALTH HISTORY OTHER REPORTS VIEWS YOUNG PEOPLE

Attention: The Chicago Public Library Wants Its Books Back!

August 15th, 2012 by Shorty

CHICAGO C P L PUBLIC LIBRARY

Yes, you read correctly. The Chicago Public Library want its books back and they won't even charge you. Well, they won't charge from August 20 – September 7, 2012. However, ***you do have to pay if you've lost an item***. Hopefully, it's just one.

If I were you, I'd take advantage of this offer for two reasons. First, hey haven't offered amnesty in over 20 years. And second, the city has been sucking the life out of residents financially, so if they are giving a inch, we better take a mile. If you have any books, videos, CDs, VCR tapes, and even cassette tapes, turn them in - no matter how long you've had them.

Your library card is pretty much like a credit card. If you don't pay your bill, your charging privileges are revoked, which is pretty much like death to me. But here's what it means to those of you who could care less about getting behind on your bills.

- You can't use the library computers when your home computer crashes
- You can't charge out movies when you can't pay your cable or NextFlix bill

Get Shorty Via E-Mail

Enter your email address:

Subscribe

Delivered by FeedBurner

Recent Posts

- Chicago Black Authors Network's 2nd Annual Urban Arts Expo – October 6, 2012
- UniverSoul Circus Will Be in Chicago Through October 21, 2012
- October 9, 2012 is the ABSOLUTE Last Day to Register to Vote
- Are You A Journalist Wondering How to Mobile Ethnic Communities to Vote?
- Social Media Week Chicago is Going on Through September 28th

Recent Comments

Shorty on Did Billy Goat Tavern Discriminate Against Us?

DON'T MISS OUT, SIGN UP TODAY

Would you like tips on how to create content that will get more shares on Facebook, Twitter, LinkedIn, Google+, YouTube, and your other social sites?

Go to www.overcomingbloggersblock.com to sign up for updates.

#50 LONG-FORM JOURNALISM

Articles exceeding 1,000 words are considered long-form journalism and are found on traditional news sites. If you decide to write these stories on a blog, use quotes, images, and other tools to make them interesting reads.

Pro:

- You can tell your story in full detail without any word limitations

Other Considerations:

- You can break long-form articles into multiple posts, which will allow you to explain your topic in full detail and give you content for several days
- Use all forms of multimedia to share your story and to vary the content on your site
- Since it is challenging to read content online for extended periods of time , give your audience options to download and print the post

SAMPLE LONG-FORM JOURNALISM POST

I wrote a long-form journalism post for Gapers Block, a popular Chicago site, about a new grocery store that opened in a food desert on the South Side of Chicago. The store not only gave a community access to fresh, healthy foods, but it also provided jobs to local residents.

AD: Calling all foodies! Try Wicker Park/Bucktown's hottest restaurants at Fall Dinner Crawl, 10-2-12. Get tickets now before they sell out! [?]

TODAY
Monday, October 1

GAPERS **** BLOCK
A WEB PUBLICATION • ESTABLISHED IN 2003 • CHICAGO, ILLINOIS

SEARCH

HOME | ARTS | BOOK CLUB | FOOD | MUSIC | POLITICS | SPORTS | ARCHIVES | NEWSLETTER | ABOUT

Drive-Thru
CHICAGO BITE BY BITE

« Sticky Sweet | Family Farmed Expo 2011 »

FEATURE MON MAR 07 2011

New Grocery Stores Bring Jobs, Access to Food

By Marcie Hill

"This is just wonderful, a wonderful surprise. Oh, I can't believe it! You hear about churches giving out stuff and everything. This has never happened in this neighborhood that I know of. Not from a store. When was the last time you heard of a store giving you twelve dollars' worth of food? Thank you."

SAMPLE CUISINE FROM SOME OF THE BEST WICKER PARK BUCKTOWN RESTAURANTS AND BARS!
THE INAUGURAL FALL DINNER CRAWL
OCTOBER 2ND, 2012 6-9PM
TICKETS: $35 in advance or $45 at the door

THE DOG SHOW MON AUG 27 2012

Neon Green Relish: A Taste Test

BY ANDREW HUFF

A Chicago-style hot dog calls for special relish -- the neon green kind. But which one is the best? We aim to find out.
Read this feature »

BLOGROLL
312 Dining Diva
A Girl in Her Kitchen
Bake & Destroy!
Blue Kitchen
Check Please! Blog
Chicagoist Food & Drink
Chicago Bites
Chicago Dining Examiner
Chicago Foodies
Chicago Gluttons
Chitown Tap
Dining Chicago
Dish
Dr. Vino

THE INAUGURAL FALL DINNER CRAWL
OCTOBER 2ND, 2012 6-9PM
SAMPLE CUISINE FROM SOME OF THE BEST WICKER PARK BUCKTOWN RESTAURANTS AND BARS!
TICKETS:
$35 in advance or

SAMPLE LONG-FORM JOURNALISM POST

Pat Arnold writes very thought-provoking long-form journalism posts on her spiritual site, The Loud Mouth in the Balcony. The placement of images makes longer stories easy to read.

Welcome to the Balcony of Life's Dramas

Drama Queen Workshops™

Up here, God Is Love

Home | DQWorkshops | Meet the Loud Mouth in the Balcony | The Loud Mouth's Blog | Concession Stand | Contact Us | Search

Either Jesus was wrong–or we are

How to live a disappointment-free life: Part 2

Overcoming Disappointment: Part 1

By loudmouthinthebalcony On May 5, 2013 · 8 Comments

Physicist Albert Einstein asserted that we cannot solve problems from the same level of consciousness at which they were created. Perhaps that's why I'm seeing an increase in requests for one-on-one Drama Queen Workshop consultations.

It appears that more of us are beginning to realize that we can't solve a problem until we fully understand it. At the current level of consciousness, some things seem absolutely incomprehensible; so it seems logical, perhaps even natural, to come at it from another vantage point.

Unquestionably, problems look starkly different when you're standing in the footlights of the world's stage than when you're sitting in the balcony. Frequently, the solutions to those problems can easily be spotted from up there, too. With that possibility in mind, we begin to look for the solutions together.

Even though each person has a different set of circumstances and concerns, I've noticed that one problem seems to arise more frequently than others: Disappointment. Many are disappointed by the situation they're in, the person they're with or the direction their lives have taken. They had a different vision and grander expectations. Therein lies the rub.

Expectation is the root of all heartache.

-William Shakespeare

Author Patricia L. Arnold, aka The "Loud Mouth in the Balcony"

Want to hear more from the Loud Mouth?

Receive each new post in your e-mailbox. Just insert your email address below:

Email Address

Subscribe!

Recent Posts

- God's favor: Spiritual truth or egoic oxymoron?
- Toppling your stumbling blocks
- Discovering your unique soul purpose
- Is forgiveness a matter of life and death?
- How to live a disappointment-free life: Part 2

NEED HELP GENERATING IDEAS?

The 62 Blog Posts to Overcome workbook can jump start your creativity and help you generate ideas for each type of post in the book.

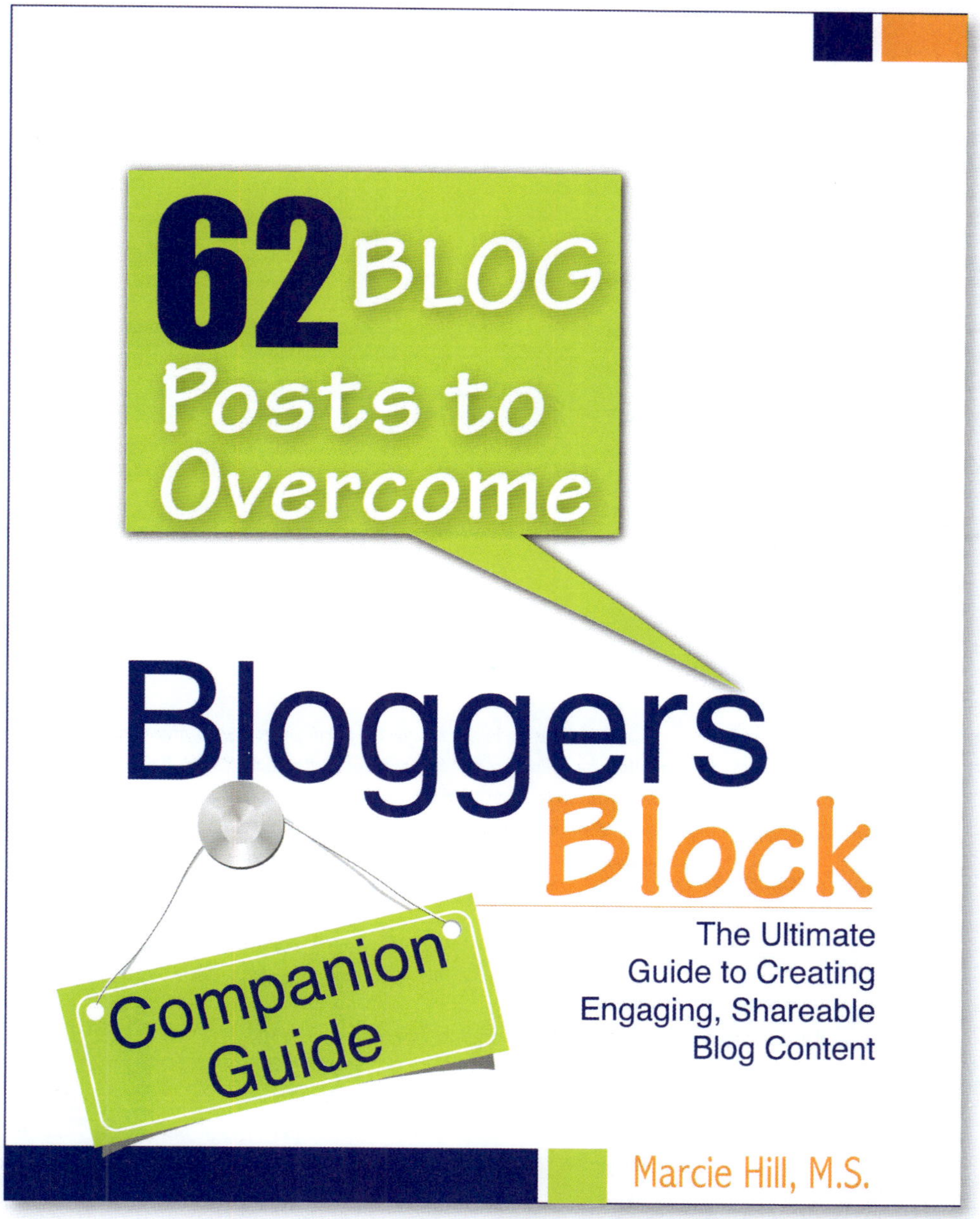

#51 EDITORIALS

Traditionally speaking, an editorial is an individual's opinion or an editor's viewpoint on a particular news story. There has been a big rise in opinion blogs over the years. Some opinions are over the top, while others are enlightening and thought-provoking.

Pros:

- Share your perspective on a topic that is relevant to your audience
- Your readers may be willing to share their opinions and perspectives as well

Other Considerations:

- Make sure your topic is well thought out and thoroughly researched
- Select one or two facts on which to share your opinion
- Criticize issues instead of people. However, if you feel the need to attack a person or a group, be ready to face the backlash that may occur

SAMPLE EDITORIAL POST

Ramsin Canon expressed what was probably on the minds of many Chicagoans in this Gapers Block article. He touched upon the political, social, economic, and real estate issues surrounding the city's racial boundaries. He also mentioned the general attitudes toward inclusion among the different racial groups.

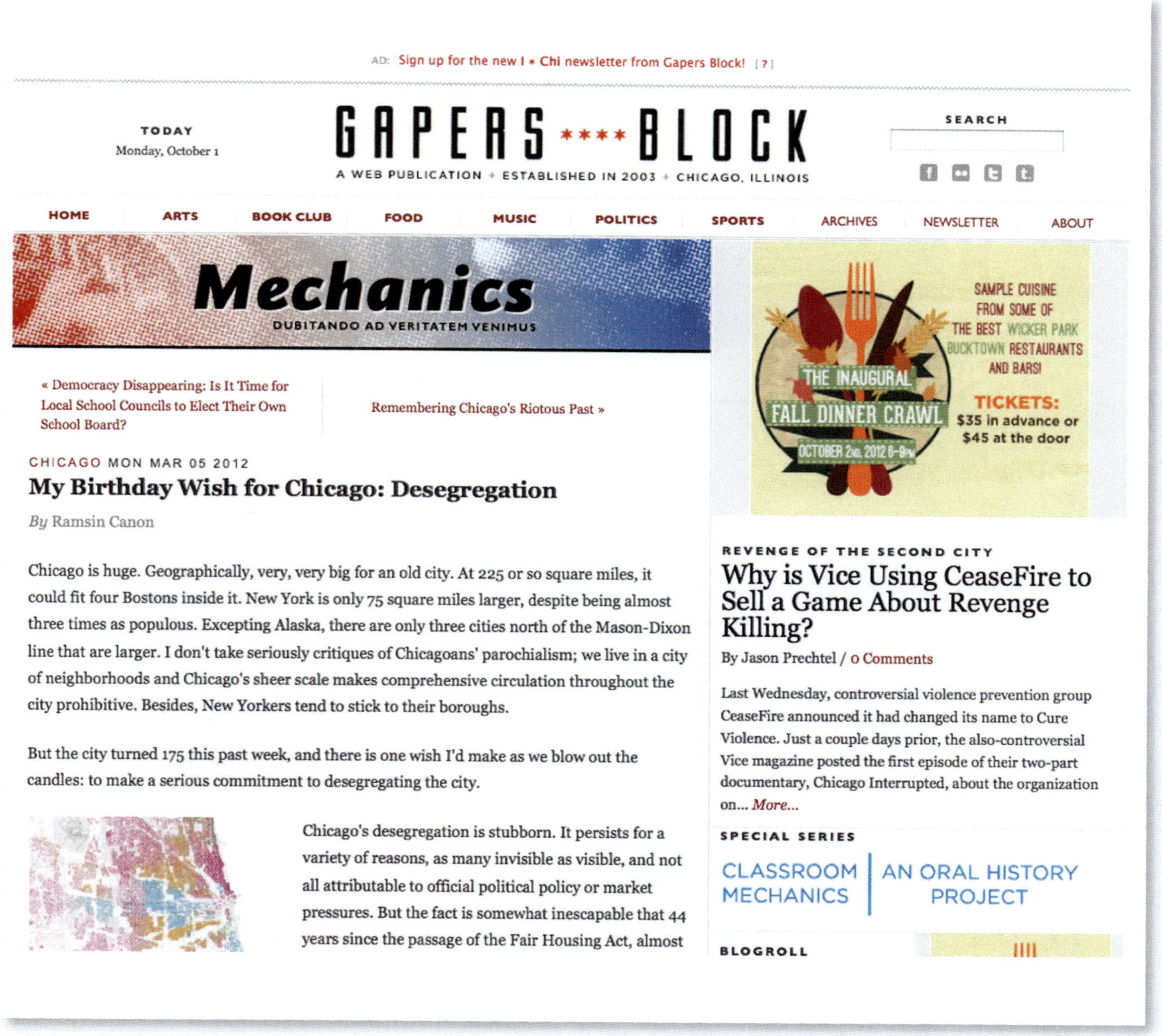

AD: Sign up for the new I ✱ Chi newsletter from Gapers Block! [?]

TODAY
Monday, October 1

GAPERS ✱✱✱✱ BLOCK
A WEB PUBLICATION ✦ ESTABLISHED IN 2003 ✦ CHICAGO, ILLINOIS

SEARCH

HOME | ARTS | BOOK CLUB | FOOD | MUSIC | POLITICS | SPORTS | ARCHIVES | NEWSLETTER | ABOUT

Mechanics
DUBITANDO AD VERITATEM VENIMUS

« Democracy Disappearing: Is It Time for Local School Councils to Elect Their Own School Board?

Remembering Chicago's Riotous Past »

CHICAGO MON MAR 05 2012

My Birthday Wish for Chicago: Desegregation

By Ramsin Canon

Chicago is huge. Geographically, very, very big for an old city. At 225 or so square miles, it could fit four Bostons inside it. New York is only 75 square miles larger, despite being almost three times as populous. Excepting Alaska, there are only three cities north of the Mason-Dixon line that are larger. I don't take seriously critiques of Chicagoans' parochialism; we live in a city of neighborhoods and Chicago's sheer scale makes comprehensive circulation throughout the city prohibitive. Besides, New Yorkers tend to stick to their boroughs.

But the city turned 175 this past week, and there is one wish I'd make as we blow out the candles: to make a serious commitment to desegregating the city.

Chicago's desegregation is stubborn. It persists for a variety of reasons, as many invisible as visible, and not all attributable to official political policy or market pressures. But the fact is somewhat inescapable that 44 years since the passage of the Fair Housing Act, almost

SAMPLE CUISINE FROM SOME OF THE BEST WICKER PARK BUCKTOWN RESTAURANTS AND BARS!
THE INAUGURAL FALL DINNER CRAWL
OCTOBER 2ND, 2012 6-8PM
TICKETS: $35 in advance or $45 at the door

REVENGE OF THE SECOND CITY

Why is Vice Using CeaseFire to Sell a Game About Revenge Killing?

By Jason Prechtel / 0 Comments

Last Wednesday, controversial violence prevention group CeaseFire announced it had changed its name to Cure Violence. Just a couple days prior, the also-controversial Vice magazine posted the first episode of their two-part documentary, Chicago Interrupted, about the organization on... *More...*

SPECIAL SERIES

CLASSROOM MECHANICS | AN ORAL HISTORY PROJECT

BLOGROLL

SAMPLE OPINION BLOG

Created by Cheryl Contee, otherwise known as Jill Tubman, Jack & Jill Politics voices the thoughts and views of the black middle class while helping to dispel mainstream media stereotypes of African Americans through education.

Like relationships, race is always a hot topic. In the post below, Cheryl writes about how race is being used in the current political climate. She also shares statistics on crimes that are committed by more white offenders when society is usually led to believe that black people are the primary offenders of most crimes.

Home Contact Info Who We Are How To Be Black

Jack & Jill Politics

A black bourgeoisie perspective on U.S. politics

21 may 2012

In the Wake of Trayvon Martin, Conservative Media Launch Race War

Author: Cheryl Contee (Jill Tubman)

IF I HAD A RACE-BAITING PRESIDENT HE WOULD LOOK JUST LIKE THIS

OWNTHEWORLD.com

Apparently the RAHOWA (short for Racial Holy War among white supremacists) hasn't come soon enough for conservatives. Didn't Glenn Beck assert that Barack Obama was planning to round up white folks and put them in concentration camps using FEMA after his election? Hmmm...hasn't happened yet but it might - under a second Obama administration, right? BuzzFeed has a takedown of the conservative media's attempt to focus on black on white crime. The truth is that crime in general is down in America while whites (and others) on Wall Street have walked scot-free despite their many crimes against black and hispanic homeowners and oh yeah, the entire global economy. Has anyone gone to jail yet for their role in the subprime mortgage crisis? I didn't think so. Right...

Oh and btw, more whites tend to get arrested for crimes than blacks in America. See the chart below. According to 2010 FBI statistics:

	Arrests	Whites		Blacks	
Robbery	25,561	12, 390	48.5%	12,878	50.4%
Larceny- theft	391,134	275,543	70.4%	108,107	27.6%
Motor Vehicle theft	18,870	13,469	72.3%	4,971	26.3%
Weapons charges	42,021	27,846	66.3%	13,650	32.5%

From BuzzFeed (thanks, Ben Smith):

search

Entries (RSS) Comments (RSS)

12187 readers BY FEEDBURNER 2878 Followers twittercounter.com

Subscribe To Email Digest

Who We Are

Cheryl Contee aka "Jill Tubman", Baratunde Thurston aka "Jack Turner", rikyrah, Leutisha Stills aka "The Christian Progressive Liberal", B-Serious, Casey Gane-McCalla, Jonathan Pitts-Wiley aka "Marcus Toussaint," Fredric Mitchell, Keith Owens, Anson Asaka, Barbara Moore, Deborah Small, Lisa Coffman, Michael Patton

Special Contributors: Rashad Robinson, Marvin Randolph, Phaedra Ellis-Lamkins, James Rucker, Rinku Sen, Adam Luna

Technical Contributor: Brandon Sheats

JJP Fellows: Krysten Clark, Chris Davis, Lauren Brown Jarvis, Justin Watts

Sponsors

Reach Millions of Liberals Daily

Sunday News and Open Thread

Boston: Rapist files for visitation rights to victim's toddler

Chris Hayes: The Republican Bubble Trap

Bruce Lisman celebrates the Galtian brilliance of Bill Stenger

Our Cat Girl comes home from the hospital

Read more...

Buy a Blogad!

Black Political Blogs

3CHICSPOLITICO

Acts of Faith In Love and Life

African-American Pundit

AfricanAmerica.org

Afro-Netizen

All About Race

Angry Black Bitch

Angry Black Lady Chronicles

Angry Black Woman

AverageBro.com

Barack Obama

Black Agenda Report Blog

Black Is, Black Ain't

www
Hey
RSS
http://
@
Wow
Hey
www.
@
RSS
http://

PART 9

HOT HOT HOT!

Hot Hot Hot! topics are the heart of heated discussions and debates. People can voice their opinions and share their expertise, which diversifies the content on your site. Additionally, these comments can become fuel for future conversations.

There are four types of Hot Hot Hot! posts that can make your site sizzle:

1. **Controversy**
2. **Rants**
3. **Debates**
4. **Critiques/Attacks**

#52 CONTROVERSY

Everyone loves controversy. You will find it posted frequently on political and entertainment blogs, as well as on social networking sites. Controversy can be an interesting diversion from the usual topics and conversations on your site.

The topics you choose do not have to be related to your site's subjects, but they should be interesting to your readers. Some people share false information to touch nerves, but you don't have to do this. Just stating facts can sometimes set off unexpected fireworks.

Pros:

- You will get different perspectives from your audience's comments
- You can turn a seemingly negative issue into a positive conversation

Other Considerations:

- You have to be able to handle the consequences of your posts, which may include negative comments and heated debates
- You may have to manage the comments and topics of discussion by frequently monitoring your readers' comments
- Be honest when providing information
- The topic, word choice, or tone that you use can incite controversy

SAMPLE CONTROVERSY POST

Politics alone is a controversial topic, but when you add socio-economic, justice, and entertainment discussions, you get a huge explosion of opinions. Readers of Chocolate City, a WWClick.com property, get all that and more.

#53 RANTS

It's okay to let off a little steam every now and then. In fact, it may good for you and your readers. It's very likely that your audience members are irritated by some of the same things that irk you. The subjects of your rants may stir up a little dissension or they may open the door to conversations and healthy debates.

Pros:

- People will feel your passion
- You may get more support on a topic than expected

Other Considerations:

- Your rant could draw negative comments
- When possible, try to put a positive spin on a negative rant
- Just in case you offend someone, be ready to defend your position
- Encourage your audience to submit their rants
- Think about what you want to write before writing it

SAMPLE RANT ON SITE

John Naisbilt said, "We are drowning in information, but starved for knowledge." Seth Godin wrote a great rant about people being "deliberately uninformed" even though they have access to unlimited information, which is usually at their fingertips. He pointed out the ways that people waste their downtime instead of filling their minds to overcome ignorance.

(click on my head)

DON'T MISS A THING
FREE UPDATES BY EMAIL

Enter your email address

me@email.com

Subscribe me! preview

powered by FeedBlitz

RSS FEEDS

Share | SUBSCRIBE BOOKMARK

Facebook: Seth's Facebook
Twitter: @thisissethsblog

SEARCH

« Killer apps now shipping (early days) | Blog Home | The shipit journal is back in stock... »

Deliberately uninformed, relentlessly so [a rant]

Many people in the United States purchase one or fewer books every year.

Many of those people have seen every single episode of American Idol. There is clearly a correlation here.

Access to knowledge, for the first time in history, is largely unimpeded for the middle class. Without effort or expense, it's possible to become informed if you choose. For less than your cable TV bill, you can buy and read an important book every week. Share the buying with six friends and it costs far less than coffee.

Or you can watch TV.

The thing is, watching TV has its benefits. It excuses you from the responsibility of having an informed opinion about things that matter. It gives you shallow opinions or false 'facts' that you can easily parrot to others that watch what you watch. It rarely unsettles our carefully self-induced calm and isolation from the world.

I got a note from someone the other day, in which she made it clear that she doesn't read non-fiction books or blogs related to her industry. And she seemed proud of this.

I was roped into an argument with someone who was sure that ear candling was a useful treatment. Had he read any medical articles on the topic? No. But he knew. Or said he did.

#54 DEBATES

You can start a debate or share an existing one by presenting topics and allowing your readers to pick a side. Also, consider allowing your readers to pick the topics, or use their comments to get conversations going.

Pros:

- By discussing issues relevant to your audience, you will engage them more
- Let people share their perspectives and introduce topics of debate

Other Considerations:

- These discussions could get heated to a point where comments may have to be moderated
- You can write a follow-up post highlighting some of the most discussed points or interesting perspectives of the debate
- Be sure to quote correctly and give credit where it is due

SAMPLE DEBATE POST

In this guest post I wrote for ProBlogger, I shared all of the reasons I feel that self-hosted blogs are more valuable than Facebook Pages. Valid arguments were made for and against both. Based on the comments, however, self-hosted blogs were favored over Facebook Pages.

Struggling to Find Time to Blog? Get Our New Productivity eBook

PROBLOGGER

HOME BLOG FORUM WORKBOOKS BOOK JOBS MAKE MONEY ARCHIVES Search Problogger... GO

Written on 4/22/2011 at 12:07 am by Guest Blogger

Why Your Self-Hosted Blog is More Valuable than Your Facebook Page

Filed Under: Social Media Tweet 515

Like 149 people like this.

This guest post is by Marcie Hill of The Write Design Company.

Facebook has taken the Web by storm in a very short period. In addition to being *the* highest ranking social networking site, it is the second most visited site in the world according to Alexa, the popular blog measuring tool. Facebook's popularity is so great that it unseated Google as the king of the Web one day in 2010.

Even though Facebook offer relationships, fun, and exposure, following are five reasons why I think your self-hosted blog is more valuable than your Facebook Page.

1. You can control your own media and space

You have limited control on Facebook. You have access to the profiles and pages you create, but having access isn't the same as ownership. And your design options are minimal. Your blog, on the other hand, is your space to do what you want, when you want, how you want. From design to set up to content.

Subscribe to the Newsletter:

Subscribe 170K readers

Join Over 321000 Readers

Earn While Snoring. Text Link Ads

Advertise on PROBLOGGER

PROBLOGGER first week of blogging

PROBLOGGER

#55 CRITIQUES/ATTACKS

A critique is a detailed or critical review of something or someone. The depth of the evaluation is the main difference between a critique and a review. Critiques become attacks when your evaluation becomes overly negative or intentionally offensive.

Pros:

- Sharing your in-depth knowledge on a topic will boost your credibility as an authority
- Your readers may have a lot to contribute to the topic

Other Considerations:

- Some topics are more sensitive than others. All you have to do is make one negative comment and you can become a "bad" person
- Choose your words carefully
- When possible, balance the critique with positive and negative perspectives
- You can't please everyone. Sometimes you have to say something negative to get people's attention. As long as it is the truth, you will be okay.
- You may be attacked in return

SAMPLE CRITIQUE POST

On my writing site, Marcie Writes, I critiqued Johnson Publications, the home of Ebony and Jet magazines, for being sold as a result of poor decision making. The communications person at the company e-mailed me and informed me that the building which housed Johnson Publications was being sold, not the company itself. I immediately updated the post with the correct the information.

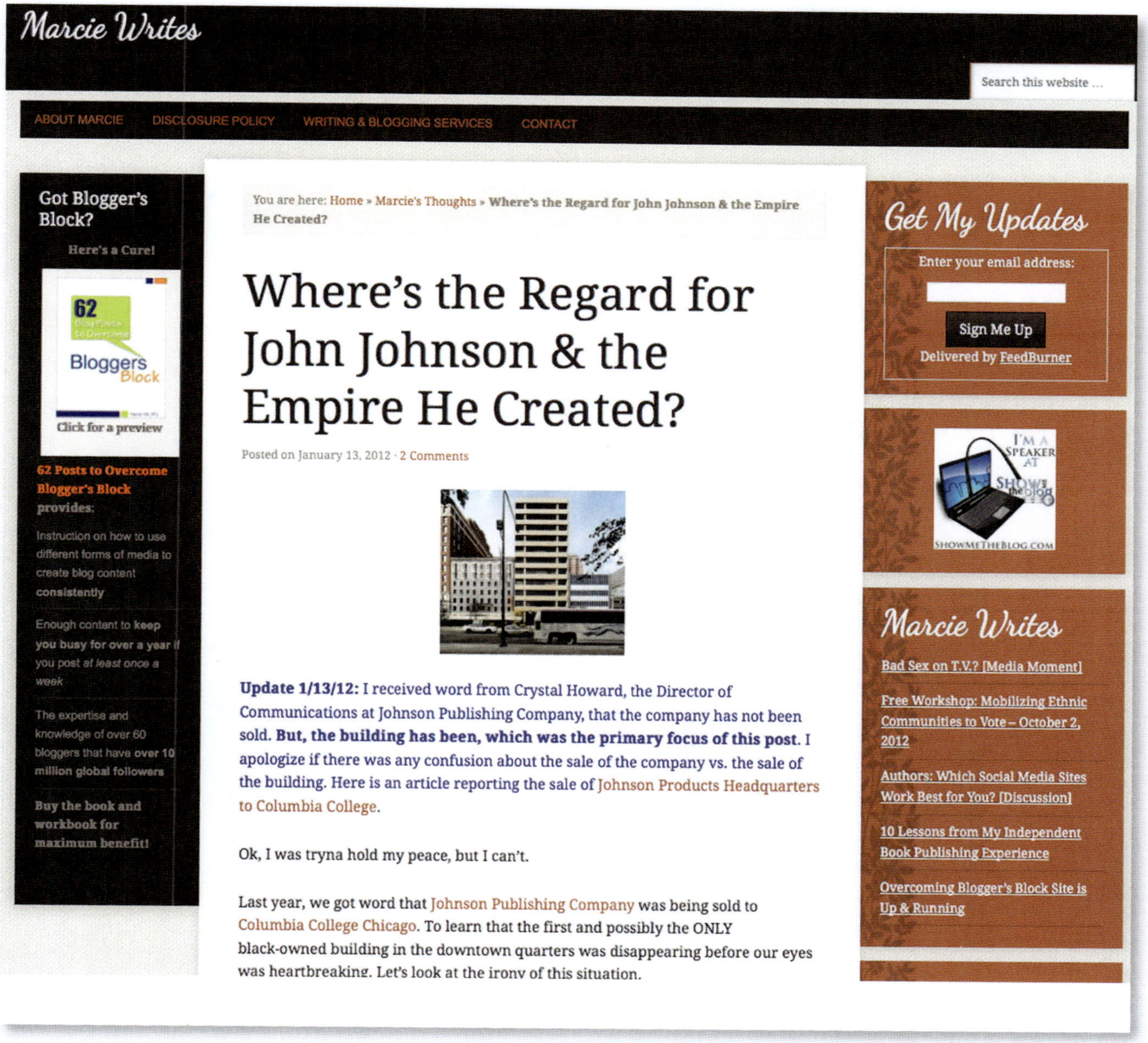
Marcie Writes

Search this website ...

ABOUT MARCIE | DISCLOSURE POLICY | WRITING & BLOGGING SERVICES | CONTACT

Got Blogger's Block?

Here's a Cure!

Click for a preview

62 Posts to Overcome Blogger's Block provides:

Instruction on how to use different forms of media to create blog content consistently

Enough content to keep you busy for over a year if you post *at least* once a week

The expertise and knowledge of over 60 bloggers that have over 10 million global followers

Buy the book and workbook for maximum benefit!

You are here: Home » Marcie's Thoughts » **Where's the Regard for John Johnson & the Empire He Created?**

Where's the Regard for John Johnson & the Empire He Created?

Posted on January 13, 2012 · 2 Comments

Update 1/13/12: I received word from Crystal Howard, the Director of Communications at Johnson Publishing Company, that the company has not been sold. **But, the building has been, which was the primary focus of this post.** I apologize if there was any confusion about the sale of the company vs. the sale of the building. Here is an article reporting the sale of Johnson Products Headquarters to Columbia College.

Ok, I was tryna hold my peace, but I can't.

Last year, we got word that Johnson Publishing Company was being sold to Columbia College Chicago. To learn that the first and possibly the ONLY black-owned building in the downtown quarters was disappearing before our eyes was heartbreaking. Let's look at the irony of this situation.

Get My Updates

Enter your email address:

Sign Me Up

Delivered by FeedBurner

Marcie Writes

Bad Sex on T.V.? [Media Moment]

Free Workshop: Mobilizing Ethnic Communities to Vote – October 2, 2012

Authors: Which Social Media Sites Work Best for You? [Discussion]

10 Lessons from My Independent Book Publishing Experience

Overcoming Blogger's Block Site is Up & Running

WANT TO READ THE FULL POST?

Go to www.overcomingbloggersblock.com to link to the actual posts in each of the categories.

PART 10
ADDITIONAL POSTS

There are two types of posts that don't really fit into any of the other categories, but they are frequently found in the blogosphere:

1. **Announcements**
2. **Income and Traffic**

#56 ANNOUNCEMENTS

Similar to boast posts, announcements allow you to share what's happening with your site or with some other aspect of your life. Announce your new site design or post about the direction your site is taking. Your audience will also love to hear about new opportunities, projects, or your personal growth. If your news requires a follow-up, be sure to do that, too. Encourage your readers to share their announcements on your site.

Pros:

- Sharing things about yourself allows your audience to connect with you more
- By being open and sharing things about yourself, your audience may be willing to do the same

Other Considerations:

- Be timely with your announcements; do not share outdated information unless it is relevant
- If an announcement requires a follow-up, be sure to do it. Don't leave people guessing about the final result of something you posted about
- Refrain from over-sharing personal information

SAMPLE ANNOUNCEMENT POST

Terrance Gaines, better known as BrothaTech, loves all things technology, especially Apple products. In this particular post, he announced the changes made by SugarSync Cloud Services; provided a brief review; included visual instructions on how to use the program; and compared similar products.

SugarSync

The Cloud storage 3-way (wait) between Dropbox, Box & SugarSync just got kicked up a notch with the entry of a completely redone SugarSync iPad App that adopts the latest queues of mobile app design and makes more use of iPad screen real estate.

First and foremost, the app has adopted the modern and simplified trend that's appearing in mobile apps. With the swipe of a finger, most if not all information is made available. This trend is definitely evident in the latest SugarSync iPad redesign.

The menu that gives you access to all of your connected Devices, Places on your device, and other locations like "Recent Documents" has been moved to a more permanent location on the left to the screen. The most used features – mobile photo and video backup are front and center on the app.

Quickly upload/backup images or access devices

Categories

- App Roundup
- Digital Lifestyle
- Events
- Featured
- Gadget Fiend
- Giveaways
- Tech Lowdown
- Why I'm Mad

GET BROTHATECH IN YOUR INBOX!
SIGN UP BELOW!

What's Your Name?

Email *

#57 INCOME AND TRAFFIC

Because very few bloggers are open to sharing how much they earn, you will see these reports on very few sites. Keep in mind that income cannot be earned without traffic, and it can take months, and sometimes years, to get both.

Pros:

- You can show other bloggers how to turn content into traffic and cash
- Use your reports as motivation to continue to build your income and site traffic

Other Considerations:

- If making money is your goal, you should create a business plan and then put your plan into action
- Be patient. It will take a while to get a consistent flow of traffic and to make money from your site

SAMPLE INCOME AND TRAFFIC REPORT

Bamidele Onibalusi, a young Internet entrepreneur, shared this report when over 10,000 people visited his site without promotion. He documented his sources of traffic, lessons learned, as well as his eBook on how to make money from blogging.

Writers in Charge
take charge of your writing career

BLOG ABOUT CONTACT BLOGGING CHALLENGE

HOME ARCHIVES BLOGGING TIPS FREELANCE WRITING GUEST BLOGGING MAKE MONEY WRITING RESOURCES

> youngprepro > My Income and Traffic Report – March 2011

My Income and Traffic Report – March 2011

By Bamidele

I made a lot of decisions when entering the new year, but the best so far is displaying my income report: not only because it helps inspire and motivate my readers but because it is what keeps me moving strongly. I also see these monthly income reports as a way to make myself accountable to my readers and in this case failure isn't an option, I'd rather not stand my income and traffic report decreasing every month.

You might have many reasons for reading these reports but my main reason for writing them is to motivate and inspire you to take action. I'd like you to know that under no circumstance am I comparing my income with that of others or using this avenue to brag because I believe we all have what we're better at and my approach is different from yours so whether you make more or less than I do has little to do with me. All I care about is having enough to spend and being happy and having a great and growing business that keeps on helping people all over the world.

Some Great News in March

A lot of great things happened in March and it seems I'm becoming happier every month.

A great thing happened in March and that was me being interviewed by supper affiliate blogger Jonathan Volk. I so much respect and look up to Jonathan and being interviewed on his blog was an honor, plus he sent me some cool traffic :). I highly recommend you read the interview here to learn some more things about me.

ABOUT WRITERS IN CHARGE

At 'Writers in Charge' our philosophy is that you, the writer, should be in charge – not your client or anybody/anything else, but you. Our goal is to help you become the person in charge.

Search this website...

A LESSON ON BLOGGING INCOME

Paul Aguiar's Money Dummy blog gives 10 common blogging lies and truths on making money from your site. Actually, his site is chock full of advice, tips, and resources about how to make money online.

DO YOU HAVE YOUR WORKBOOK?

Don't delay. Go to www.overcomingbloggersblock.com to get your workbook today.

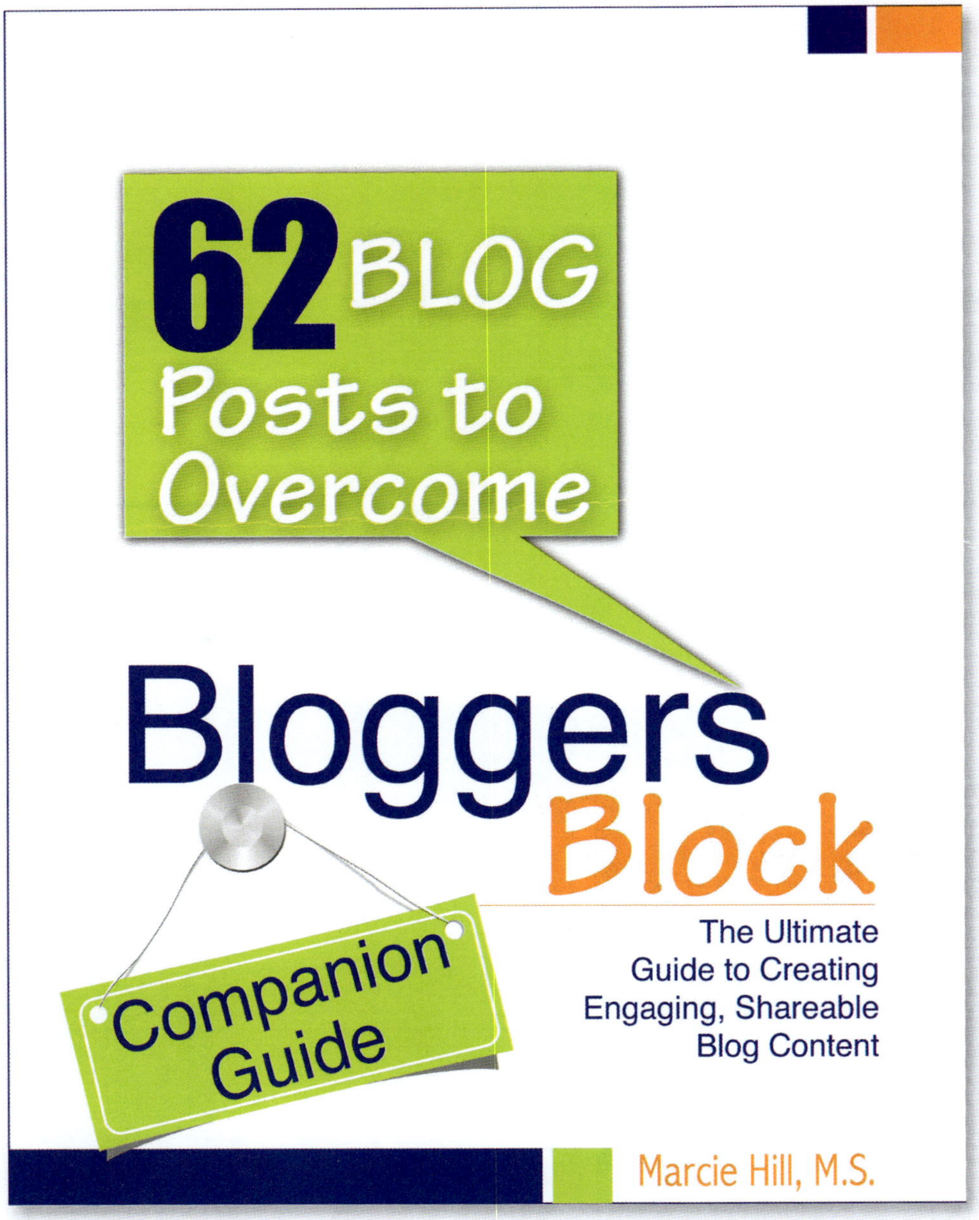

PART 11
ROUNDING IT UP

This is where you compile your research, data, posts, and other information to create comprehensive reports, books, and other products to give away or sell. There are five ways to round up your information:

1. **"Best Of" and "Top" Posts**
2. **Case Studies**
3. **Series**
4. **Books**
5. **Repurposed Content**

#58 "BEST OF" AND "TOP" POSTS

"Best of" or "Top" posts are popular posts where you gather the coolest or most thought-provoking content either from your site or from other sources to create an informative list.

Pros:

- Link and list posts are fairly easy to create on those days that you are experiencing blogger's block
- You will increase your credibility as a resource and possibly build relationships through linking

Other Considerations:

- Share information that is relevant to your audience. Better yet, take time to spotlight the sites and ventures of your readers
- Use multimedia tools to relay your information

SAMPLE "TOP" POST

Fetching Friday – Resources & Mashup is a signature link post on Kristi Hines's Kikolani site. The comprehensive post below shares links to "the best posts of the week in blogging, business, freelancing, SEO, and social media."

kikolani

Marketing Strategies for Business and Professional Bloggers

Want Traffic and Engagement?
Learn How to Promote Your Content Effectively

BPP

HOME ABOUT FREELANCE WRITING SERVICES SOCIAL MEDIA CONSULTING LATEST POSTS ADVERTISE CONTACT

Top 10 Things That Can Hurt Your Blog

June 3, 2010 by Arie

Tweet 44 Buffer 0 Like 18 g+1 3 Share Pin it

This guest post was written by Arie Rich, Editor of KMP Blog.

Blogging for two plus years I have played around with stuff to see what works and doesnâ€™t for my blog. I have tried every item on this list and this has brought me to share with you the top 10 things that can hurt your blog in the long run, from a KMP perspective.

1. The Blogroll

I am not a huge fan of the blogroll. There are pros and cons about having one. One of the pros is that you can direct traffic to your blog if you are listed on someone elseâ€™s blogroll which can help increase your rank. The con is if someone's rank is not as high as yours, having them on your blogroll could hurt your rank. So I choose not to have a blogroll.

2. Lack of Interaction with Readers

I believe blogger/reader interaction is a major plus. Simple ways to do this is by replying to comments left on your blog, as well as interacting via other social networks such as Twitter, Facebook, etc. The more interaction with your readers, you have the more loyal their readership will be.

3. Loud Layout or Background

Nothing annoys me more than a loud, busy background or confusing layout. Having a busy background gets overwhelming for the reader which can lead to quick exits and high bounce rates.

4. Music Players and Auto Playlist

There is nothing like a good olâ€™ music player, playing your favorite tunes, while reading your amazing blog. Ummâ€¦ I donâ€™t think so. I have nothing against music, but having an automatic music playing on your site can drive people away. Not everyone might like the music on your playlist, especially if you are having it auto play. If your blog is private then by all means have a music player, itâ€™s your blog. But if your blog is public, you need to be more conscious of your readers. Your blog is not just for you but for others, so choose wisely.

5. Poor Layout

Have you ever visited a blog that has amazing articles but their layout is just not â€œreader/visitor friendly?â€ I have. I am not saying you should spend a fortune on a background, but the first thing people notice when visiting your site is your layout, then your work. Layouts that compliment the articles that you write make a great combo and will have your readers complimenting your great work as well as your amazing site. Compliments lead to referrals which leads to more traffic.

Write a Book
and Make it a Big Success
FREE video with tips from Jack Canfield, who has created 47 New York Times® Bestselling Books
Watch the video now

Subscribe today to receive the latest updates from Kikolani and news for successful personal, professional, and business bloggers! You will also receive my free 8,000+ word guide on guest blogging!

THE GUEST BLOGGING SURVIVAL GUIDE
SECRETS TO BECOMING A PROLIFIC GUEST BLOGGER TO INCREASE AUTHORITY, FANS, AND TRAFFIC
KRISTI HINES

Enter your email address...

STAY INFORMED

#59 CASE STUDIES

A case study is an extensive study of people, events, places, or systems to determine the success, failure, or change over a period of time.

Pros:

- You will gain insights into how things work, what makes them function successfully (or not), and how you can apply them to your life
- You can boost your skills in writing case studies
- You may become an authority on the topics on which you're reporting

Other Considerations:

- You will spend an extensive amount of time researching and reporting results
- Some topics require cooperation from other people, so be patient and tactful
- You can give your audience assignments to help gather this information

SAMPLE CASE STUDY SITE

Social Media Examiner, "the world's largest online social media magazine, is designed to help businesses discover how to best use social media tools like Facebook, Google+, Twitter and LinkedIn to connect with customers, generate more brand awareness and increase sales." Thus, the case studies provide practical tips and resources on how to build and maximize your social media presence, as well as how to make money.

#60 SERIES

A number of blog posts with similar topics posted at different times is considered a series. Your articles can be posted hourly, daily, or weekly. You can start a series and allow your readers to contribute through guest posts or develop a mini-course.

Pros:

- Boost your expert status by sharing your knowledge
- Your readers may submit guest posts relevant to the topics, which will increase their visibility and credibility as an authority in their respective subjects

Other Considerations:

- Series are sometimes accidental, but are usually planned
- Depending on the topic, a post series can be time-consuming to develop
- Use multimedia tools to share information
- Your series could become a podcast, videoblog, or Internet TV show

SAMPLE SERIES POST

John Saddington gathered the most relevant posts to create a blog series for his readers on Tent-blogger. The posts were selected based on subject matter, timeliness, or other commonalities.

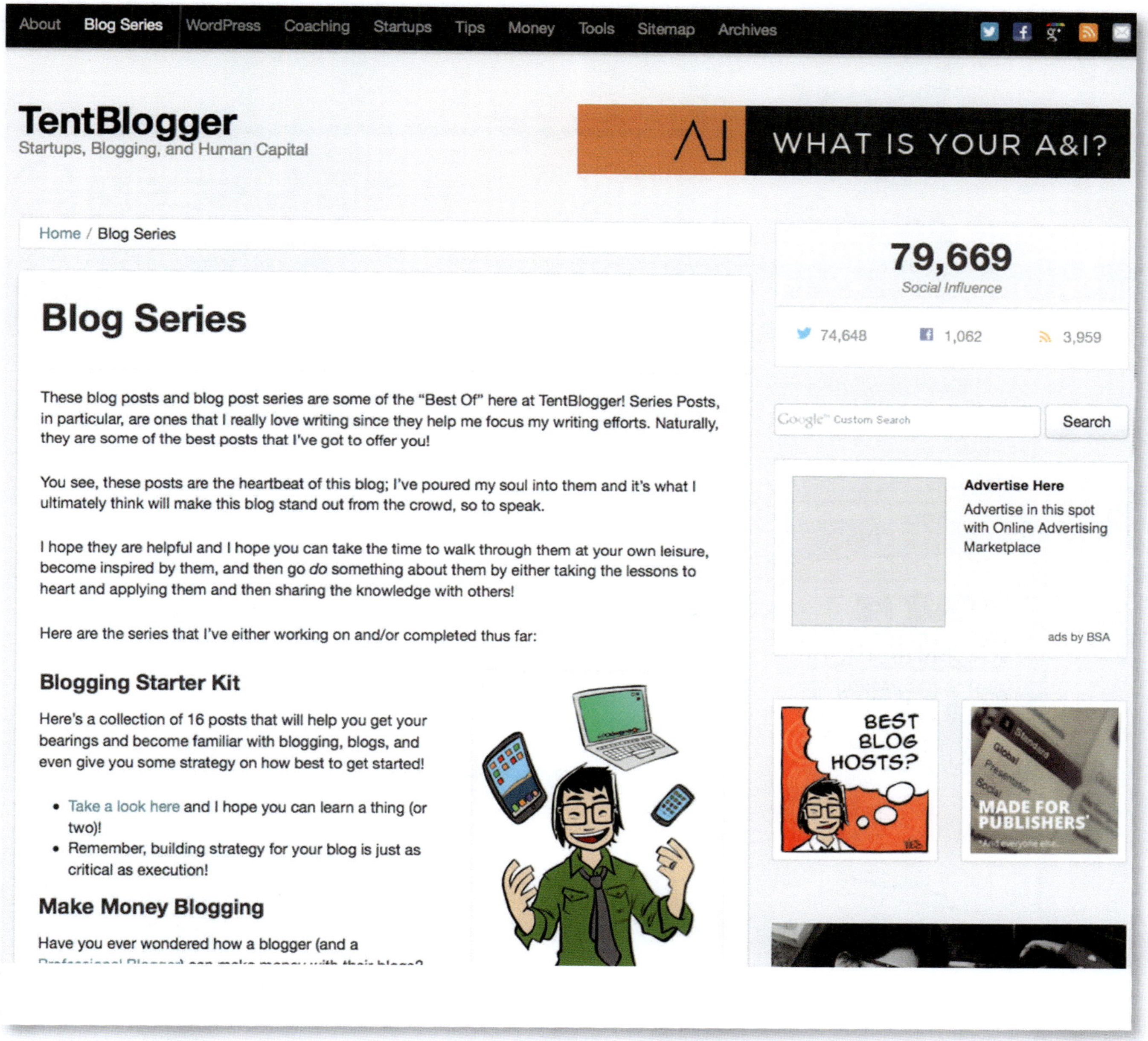

About | Blog Series | WordPress | Coaching | Startups | Tips | Money | Tools | Sitemap | Archives

TentBlogger
Startups, Blogging, and Human Capital

WHAT IS YOUR A&I?

Home / Blog Series

Blog Series

These blog posts and blog post series are some of the "Best Of" here at TentBlogger! Series Posts, in particular, are ones that I really love writing since they help me focus my writing efforts. Naturally, they are some of the best posts that I've got to offer you!

You see, these posts are the heartbeat of this blog; I've poured my soul into them and it's what I ultimately think will make this blog stand out from the crowd, so to speak.

I hope they are helpful and I hope you can take the time to walk through them at your own leisure, become inspired by them, and then go *do* something about them by either taking the lessons to heart and applying them and then sharing the knowledge with others!

Here are the series that I've either working on and/or completed thus far:

Blogging Starter Kit

Here's a collection of 16 posts that will help you get your bearings and become familiar with blogging, blogs, and even give you some strategy on how best to get started!

- Take a look here and I hope you can learn a thing (or two)!
- Remember, building strategy for your blog is just as critical as execution!

Make Money Blogging

Have you ever wondered how a blogger (and a

79,669
Social Influence

74,648 | 1,062 | 3,959

Google Custom Search | Search

Advertise Here
Advertise in this spot with Online Advertising Marketplace

ads by BSA

#61 BOOKS

Currently, there is a trend of turning blogs into books of all formats: traditional, self-published, audio, and eBooks. There are companies and services that make publishing in all of these formats very easy.

Pros:

- The content is already created
- You already have an audience that likes your work

Other Considerations:

- Be sure to hire a professional editor and designer for your published and electronic books
- Submit your work to the Copyright Office. This is a small investment in order to protect your intellectual property
- Survey your audience to find out if they are willing to buy your book and for how much
- Time, money, and control are the main considerations when considering publishing options
- Some bloggers have gotten book deals with major publishers because of the content and topics on their sites

SAMPLE BOOK FROM POSTS

A few years ago, ProBlogger Darren Rowse gave his audience assignments through a project he created called "31 Days to Build a Better Blog." These projects became a published book in 2010. It is now a second edition publication and is available in traditional and electronic book formats.

#62 REPURPOSED CONTENT

You can repurpose the content on your site and make money from it depending on your goals. With the exception of people whose blogs are their businesses or for those people who sell advertising, there are very few people who are paid directly for the content they create on their sites. Thus, repurposing content is a way to get paid and increase your authority as a subject matter expert.

Here are a few ways to repurpose your content:

- Turn your newsletter into an audio format and share it as a podcast
- Turn your text into audio and video formats
- Transcribe your audio and video into text
- Use your content for speeches at events
- Create books and eBooks from your content
- Create photobooks from images
- Make slideshows and screencasts from your content

Pros:

- Content is readily available
- You can get paid for the content if you choose to sell it
- You will gain new skills with each new software program you utilize to produce content
- Your expertise will be shared with a broader audience because you are offering the public different options to access your message

Other Considerations:

- Be sure to organize your content. Revisions and editing will be needed regardless of which repurposing option you choose
- You have to market beyond your immediate site
- You may experience a spike in traffic on your site, which could convert into dollars for you
- Many of the tools needed to create these various products are free. You just have to invest time and creativity

A LESSON ON REPURPOSING CONTENT

Anyone who has ever thought about creating informational products of any kind needs to listen to this audio interview between Robert Bruce and Ben Settle on Copyblogger. They discuss why you should consider selling products, how to create them, and ways to market and sell your goods.

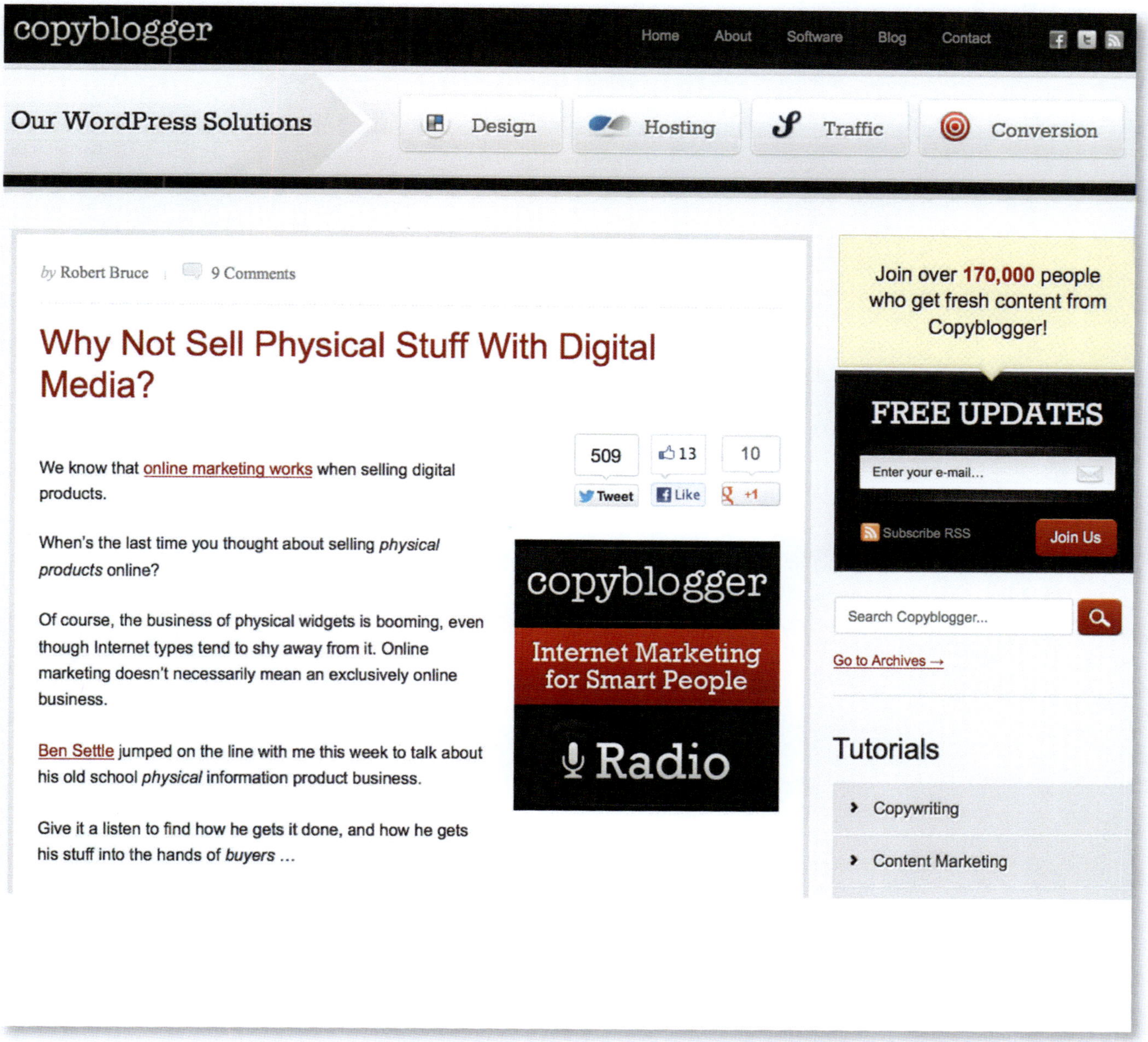

CONCLUSION

You have just learned about the 62 types of posts that will help you overcome blogger's block. There are more than enough examples to keep you busy for an entire year if you post at least once a week. For content creators who post frequently, this is an opportunity to expand your creativity and gain new skills. The posts presented in this book can apply to traditonal blogs, microblogs like Twitter and Tumbler, as well as status updates on your social networking sites.

To kick start your creativity and to help you develop a consistent routine, visit www.overcomingbloggerblock.com to:

- Sign up to receive updates about new products, trainings, and workshops
- Get tips, tools, and resources on how to overcome this horrible condition
- Obtain step-by-step instruction on how to produce the different types of posts
- Purchase the 62 Block Posts to Overcome Blogger's Block Companion Guide
- Purchase additional copies of the book and companion guide

Feel free to contact me at msmarcie@overcomingbloggersblock.com to share how your blogging life has changed as a result of applying new or different types of posts to your site.

Have fun and unleash your creativity!

FEATURED BLOGGERS

The bloggers presented here are listed in the order in which they appear in the book. Be sure to check out their sites for more knowledge and resources on blogging, social media, writing, business, and other interests.

Vernessa Taylor	Coach Notes Blog	www.localbusinesscoachonline.com
Ben Barden	Quick Blog Tips	www.quickblogtips.com
Marcie Hill	The Write Design Company	www.overcomingbloggersblock.com
Ileane Smith	Basic Blog Tips	www.basicblogtips.com
Clara Freeman	Authentic Woman	www.authentic-woman.net
Vikram Roy	Vikram Roy's Blog	www.vikramroyblog.wordpress.com
Marcie Hill	Real Skate Stories	www.realskatestories.com
John Chow	John Chow	www.johnchow.com
Daniel Scocco	Daily Blog Tips	www.dailyblogtips.com
Kiesha Easley	We Blog Better	http://weblogbetter.com
Peggy Stevenson	Chicago Daily Photoblog	www.ps-chicagodailyphoto.blogspot.com
Gary Vaynerchuk	Wine Library TV	http://tv.winelibrary.com
Mitch Mitchell	TT Mitchell Consulting	www.ttmitchellconsulting.com/Mitchblog
Liz Strauss	Liz Strauss	www.lizstrauss.com
Electra Ford	Virtual Office Center	www.virtualofficecenter.net
Chris Brogan	Chris Brogan	www.chrisbrogan.com
Jay Willingham	Daily Infographics	http://dailyinfographic.com
Denise Wakeman	Denise Wakeman	www.denisewakeman.com
Martin Lindsey	Martin Lindsey	www.martinlindsey.com
James Gorman	Women Worth Watching	www.womenworthwatching.com
Jennifer Brown Banks	Pen & Prosper	www.penandprosper.blogspot.com
Gail Gardner	Grow Map	www.growmap.com
Ching Ya	Social@BloggingTracker	www.wchingya.com
Jayme Soulati	Soulati	www.soulati.com/blog
Aminah Hanan	Michelle Obama Watch	www.michelleobamawatch.com
Luvvie Ajayi	Red Pump Project	www.theredpumpproject.org
Marcie Hill	Shorty	www.goshorty.net
Sharon Hurley Hall	Get Paid to Write Online	www.getpaidtowriteonline.com
Melinda Emerson	Succeed As Your Own Boss	www.succeedasyourownboss.com
Dequiana Jackson	Entrepreneurs Resources	www.entrepreneur-resources.net
Danny Iny	Firepole Marketing	www.firepolemarketing.com
Internet Design Zone	Fun Quiz Cards	www.funquizcards.com
Sherryl Perry	Keep Up with the Web	www.keepupwiththeweb.com
Phil Bowne	Rhetoric Robot	www.roboticrhetoric.wordpress.com
Joel Falcone	Fuel Your Blogging	www.fuelyourblogging.com
Marcie Hill	The Write Design Company	www.thewritedesignco.com
Amy Clark	Mom Advice	www.momadvice.com
Susie & Otto Collins	Love and Relationship Advice	www.susieandotto.com
Hesham Zebida	Famous Bloggers	www.famousbloggers.net
Justin Germino	Dragon Blogger	www.dragonblogger.com
Davide Jones	Blogging Pro	www.bloggingpro.com
Jane Sheeba	ProBlogging Success	www.probloggingsuccess.com
Scott Winterroth	Country Music Chicago	www.countrymusicchicago.com
Anne Wayman	About Freelance Writing	www.aboutfreelancewriting.com
KeriLynn Engel	Amazing Women in History	www.amazingwomeninhistory.com
A.G.	Regected Riter	www.regectedriter.wordpress.com
Contact	The Onion	www.theonion.com

FEATURED BLOGGERS

Second City Cop	Second City Cop	http://secondcitycop.blogspot.com
Phil Barry	Crunchy Crunchy Biscuits	crunchycrunchybiscuits.com
Vladimir Nesterenko	Smilezilla	www.smilezilla.com
Patrick Boylan	Welles Bulldog	www.wellesparkbulldog.com
Marcie Hill	Shorty: Your Chicago South Side Resource	www.goshorty.net
Andrew Huff	Gapers Block	www.gapersblock.com
Pat Arnold	Loud Mouth in the Balcony	www.loudmouthinthebalcony.com
Andrew Huff	Gapers Block	www.gapersblock.com
Cheryl Contee	Jack &Jill Politics	www.jackandjillpolitics.com
Charles Mambo	Chocolate City	www.chocolatecity.cc
Seth Godin	Seth Godin	www.sethgodin.com/sg
Darren Rowse	ProBlogger	www.problogger.net
Marcie Hill	Marcie Writes	www.marciewrites.com
Terrance Gaines	BrothaTech	www.brothatech.com
Bamidele Onibalusi	YoungPrePro	www.youngprepro.com
John Aguiar	Money Dummy Blog	www.johnpaulaguiar.com
Kristi Hines	Kikolani	www.kikolani.com
Michael Stelzner	Social Media Examiner	www.socialmediaexaminer.com
John Saddington	Tent Blogger	www.tentblogger.com
Darren Rowse	ProBlogger	www.problogger.net
Robert Bruce	Copy Blogger	www.copyblogger.com

ABOUT THE AUTHOR

Marcie Hill, M.S., is an accomplished freelance writer, blog addict and social media enthusiast with over twelve years of experience writing for businesses and publications.

Her published successes have appeared in international, national and local print and online publications, including *Forbes*, *Toastmaster* magazine, *St. Louis* magazine and the *Chicago Independent Bulletin* community newspaper, ProBlogger, Basic Blog Tips, BlogWorld, About Freelance Writing, and Write to Done.

Lastly, she owns four blogs; has self-published four eBooks; and has presented at national and local blogging and social media conferences, including New Media Expo, Social Media Week and Blogging While Brown.

NOTES AND IDEAS

Printed in Dunstable, United Kingdom

91343458R00098